THE LITTLE HERO

THE LITTLE HERO

ONE BOY'S FIGHT FOR FREEDOM

IQBAL MASIH'S STORY

ANDREW CROFTS

First published in 2006 by Vision Paperbacks,
a division of Satin Publications Ltd
101 Southwark Street
London SE1 0JF
UK
info@visionpaperbacks.co.uk
www.visionpaperbacks.co.uk
Publisher: Sheena Dewan

A catalogue record for this book is available from the British Library.

ISBN-13: 978-1-904132-84-4
ISBN-10: 1-904132-84-7

2 4 6 8 10 9 7 5 3 1

Cover photo: EMPICS
Cover and text design by ok?design
Printed and bound in the UK by Mackays of Chatham Ltd,
Chatham, Kent

To Riff, a man who makes things happen.

'The moment a slave resolves that he will
no longer be a slave, his fetters fall.
He frees himself and shows the way to others.
Freedom and slavery are mental states.'
Gandhi, Non-Violence in Peace and War, *1949*

'In giving freedom to the slave,
we assure freedom to the free.'
Abraham Lincoln, Annual Message to Congress, 1862

'To die will be an awfully big adventure.'
J M Barrie, Peter Pan, *1928*

CONTENTS

CHAPTER ONE

AN HONOURED VISITOR

'Don't go back to the city, stay another day,' Iqbal's mother pleaded. Iqbal was glad that he'd returned to the village. His mother was full of maternal pride, revelling in the excitement of the occasion. This was only his second visit but both times he had attracted crowds of people to the house bearing gifts of drinks and food.

He knew his mother, Inayat, had no idea what her small son did when he was in Lahore, but she was pleased to enjoy the attention and respect that he brought to her door. God knows she deserved it after all she'd been through; the endless work and struggle and a husband so useless to her she'd have been better off on her own from the start.

Iqbal also knew she'd never given a thought to what he'd been doing all those years when he went off to work in the carpet factory, either. Why would she? She had enough to worry about as it was. The carpet master had assured her he would look after her son like an uncle. How would she know to distrust the word of a man who was always so friendly towards her?

'I have to get back, Mama,' he told her, wriggling forward to the edge of the bed where he'd been holding court, his feet still swinging above the ground, reminding her that however important her son might now be in the world, he was still just a child. 'My medication is in the city. I mustn't miss it, even for one day.'

The relatives and neighbours sitting with him on the bed shifted reluctantly to let him through. They immediately sprawled out to fill the space he'd left beneath the lazy ceiling fan. It had been a pleasant afternoon for them all, neighbours and relatives alike, with Iqbal's visit to distract them from their daily problems and Inayat's hospitality to spoil them with endless cups of tea.

Iqbal cast his eyes round his family home. It seemed so much more basic now he had experienced more of the world. The house consisted of two cramped, windowless rooms leading onto an enclosed courtyard with an open kitchen and a basic toilet in the opposite corner. The contents of the toilet emptied themselves out through the front wall of the courtyard into the open sewer, which ran along the edge of the narrow alleyway outside. All the houses in the village were the same, endless plain stone walls, punctuated with a variety of makeshift gates and doors, guarding the privacy of the families that gathered inside to talk and argue, drink tea and complain. Or simply sit still and try to keep cool.

The walls of the rooms were lined with shelves displaying rows of lovingly washed and polished tin cups, plates and glasses. Every possession a family had in Muridke was on show for visitors to admire. There was nowhere else to store anything anyway. Large tin trunks protected clothes from the dust and the humidity, and from insects that would have destroyed them long before anyone could have afforded to replace them.

Iqbal was proud, and a little embarrassed, to see that most of the pictures propped up around the shelves were of him. Some had been cut from newspapers and others had been given to the family as gifts by visitors who had come to the village eager to see where Iqbal started life. The biggest newspaper cutting was already curling up from the heat and yellowing at the edges. It carried a grainy picture of him standing on a podium with his arms stretched up as if accepting applause, a rare smile of pure joy vanquishing the lines of concentration that usually furrowed his brow. He remembered the moment that was taken, in Stockholm, thousands of miles away from Muridke.

There was no need for windows in these houses, the light outside was relentless and blinding, an enemy to be kept out rather than a friend to be encouraged in. A set of steps curved up over the kitchen leading to the roof, where there was no protection from the baking heat of the sun. The village roofs were an alternative stone landscape, interlaced by the network of alleys that barely separated the houses, and by precariously stacked towers of birdcages containing lovingly bred homing pigeons.

Children of the village treated the roofs as an extension of their playgrounds in the streets and canals, shouting to one another across the alleys as they worked at getting stubborn kites up into the hot thermals, which brought almost no movement to the air near the ground. Sometimes a child would become over-excited or over-absorbed in the challenge and run too close to an unguarded edge, or would knock against a wall that had been hastily stacked with dry bricks, and would topple down, badly injuring or even killing itself on the pathways below.

The bereaved family would mourn briefly and move on, one less mouth to feed, but still plenty left behind. When there are so many dangers in a family's life it's impossible to guard against misfortune. God's will could not be thwarted simply by taking a few precautions, everyone knew that. What would be would be – God willing!

Hopping down off the bed, Iqbal went round the room solemnly shaking hands with all the men and boys, leaning across the bed to reach the ones sprawled at the back against the wall, his face screwed up in a tight, serious frown as he concentrated on missing no one. Iqbal had always been a very respectful boy.

Other relatives, mostly female, were sitting around in the courtyard, unable to get into the rooms. Sobya, his little sister, smiled shyly as she saw him come out. He was sorry that she no longer ran up to hug him as she had when she was tiny. He squeezed her hand and said goodbye, and her smile broadened a little more.

His old companions were waiting around the gate for him to emerge, having been shooed out of the house by the older women. Two boys pushed their way out of the crowd to be at his side, his cousin Liaqat and his friend Faryad.

Liaqat's father was Inayat Bibi's brother, Amanat, a farm worker out in the fields between Muridke and Lahore. Iqbal was now planning to break his journey back to the city and go with the other boys to see his uncle. He hadn't originally intended to do so, knowing it would make him very late back, but his cousin had persuaded him.

'It will make the journey much longer,' Iqbal had protested.

'You'll still be back in Lahore in time to take your medicine,' Liaqat argued. 'My father would like to see you. He's always loved you.'

Iqbal smiled. Liaqat had always known the way to his heart.

Although he'd never been good at playing children's games, Iqbal enjoyed being with Liaqat and Faryad because they expected nothing of him. They weren't interested in what might have happened to Iqbal in the city or where he had travelled to in the aeroplane. They didn't bother to question why so many people wanted to see him and shake his hand when he came back to visit, or why he was allowed to sit with the adults of the village when they were chased away, but they were willing to wait until he was free to play with them again. They bore him no ill will, he was Iqbal; he had always been different from everyone else.

As the three boys made their way along the alley, between the foul-smelling drains, a crowd of smaller children danced around them, aware that a visit from Iqbal made the day somehow special, even if they didn't know why. Everyone told stories about him, each person wanting to add another layer of wonder in order to enjoy the looks of amazement on the faces of their listeners. No one really cared any more where the truth lay, they just liked the idea that someone from their own village, someone they could claim kinship to, was a legend. Maybe, some of them wondered, if a few more people in high places got to hear the name of the village someone in authority might do something about the drains. Iqbal wore his celebrity with dignity; he responded to any comment that was addressed to him, and shook any hand that was proffered, never in too much of a hurry to pass the time of day.

The streets that had once seemed such a maze of towering walls seemed mean and constricting to him now that he had travelled to big cities and seen Europe and America.

They emerged from the stuffy shade of the alley and were hit by the full heat of the late afternoon sun. More boys were diving in and out of the brick-coloured waters of the canal, ignoring the buffaloes that wallowed around them, only their horns, eyes, nostrils and the ridges of their spines showing above the refreshing, rusty liquid. Others in the group around Iqbal were unable to resist the temptation and dived in fully clothed, vanishing from sight for a few seconds before emerging with their shirts and trousers clinging to their glistening skins, rejoining the chattering, smiling group as if they'd never left it, steaming gently.

The priest at the tiny Christian church beside the canal was still closing up and talking to the last of the Easter worshippers as Iqbal ran over to shake his hand and say goodbye. The priest ruffled his hair and smiled. There was something about Iqbal's earnestness that encouraged adults to smile and to feel just a twinge of discomfort, as if his serious brown eyes were staring straight through into their souls.

'Come back and see us soon,' the priest said.

'I'll try,' Iqbal assured him, 'but there's so much to do in Lahore with my school work and helping Ehsan. I've got to work really hard so I can pass the college tests for America.'

'We understand,' the priest said. 'You're needed in so many places, and you must never neglect your education.'

'Yes. Education is the most important thing there is,' Iqbal agreed. 'Without it no one can be truly free.'

The priest ruffled his hair again and nodded his farewell. Iqbal and his two friends ran off to catch up with an older boy who was driving a donkey cart. They jumped on the back to save themselves the long walk up to the main road.

The driver of the cart laughed as they joined him and whipped the poor bedraggled donkey hard to make it go faster. The welcome breeze made his long shirt billow out behind him as he stood with his bare feet braced on the boards, the reins loose in his hand, perfectly balanced from years of practice. The three passengers sat on the back of the flat cart, the vibration from the wheels below making them bounce uncomfortably. It would have been less painful to stand like their driver, but they lacked his confidence.

As they rumbled closer to the main road the traffic built up and the crowds at the sides of the road grew denser around the food stalls. As the heat of the day relented a little, men and boys who had been sleeping in the ragged buildings behind the stalls, or simply sheltering from the sun, started to make their way back out into the light, only to sit down again on the first available surface. Everywhere men lounged around, drinking tea and talking. The boys shouted greetings to faces they recognised, some of whom shouted back.

'It's Iqbal, my famous cousin from the city,' Liaqat called out and Iqbal smiled and waved politely.

Some of the men were doing business and here and there a woman or girl moved amongst them, shopping or helping with the cooking. The cart wove between the lorries, motorbikes and rickshaws, the donkey apparently as unconcerned about the chaos as everyone else, trusting to luck. If God willed it they would be spared an accident.

The driver pulled the cart up beside a tea stall where his brothers were gathered. It seemed this was the end of the free ride, although nothing was said, so Iqbal and his friends splashed down into a patch of mud created by someone's wastewater, and continued their journey on foot. Iqbal never grew tired of watching the world go by. The other two boys teased one another, occasionally pushing and slapping each other in play, but neither interfered with Iqbal's train of thought. Although he was their age he had the aura of someone much older and wiser, someone who deserved respect. Iqbal didn't notice their horseplay going on around him, his face serious with concentration as he took in everything he saw. His mind was churning over and over, trying to make sense of the messy world he'd been born into. Ehsan had taught him how to see things through different eyes.

The main road to Lahore came into sight. The traffic was thicker and faster than on the side road to Muridke, and the horns louder and more insistent. Despite its size it was no more disciplined than the smaller road had been. On the other side of the dual carriageway the boys could see a bus approaching, which would take them to the end of the track leading out into the fields to Amanat's house.

'Quick or we'll miss it!' Iqbal shouted and ran out into the traffic with the other two close on his heels. The blare of horns increased all around as drivers swerved past them from both directions. No one slowed down or tried to hold the boys back. They reached the central reservation, where the authorities had erected a barrier in a vain effort to persuade the drivers to stay on the right side of the road and to dissuade pedestrians from crossing. They repeated their dance with death to reach the other side, just in time to join the crowd pushing their way onto the already full bus.

It seemed impossible that any more people could force their way into the solidly packed mass of hot, sweating bodies, but everyone did. By pushing his way through the legs of the standing adults, Iqbal managed to reach one of the open windows, resting his chin on the ledge and breathing deeply at the relatively fresh air, the bodies of the other passengers crushed around him, his eyes the only part of him still able to move, watching the passing scenery as the driver tried to gather some speed with his load. The elderly engine grumbled noisily and farted black fumes over the motorbikes that swarmed in its wake. The bikes accelerated away and past, despite being laden down with whole families, more people than the manufacturers could ever have dreamed possible when they designed the machines.

The crowds of people thinned out as the bus travelled away from the road junction, replaced by the occasional factory or brick kiln backing on to open, deserted countryside. When the bus grunted and hissed to a halt at the track they needed, the boys fought their way off, laughing at the indignant shouts of the women they had to push out of the way to get to the door. As the bus drew away from them and the other disembarked passengers went their own ways, the traffic became just a passing stream and a sort of peacefulness settled on the boys. The further up the track they walked, past a local school building and some makeshift warehouses, the more distant the sound of the traffic became. The single line of buildings on either side of the track was less busy than those on the road to Muridke, because this was a road to nowhere. The one-room houses and shops grew more sporadic as they went, until eventually they were past the last one and into open countryside.

It was like coming up for air. There were no cars or motorbikes, no people and the only houses were the ones in the small rural settlements, way in the distance across the open land. The grass had been grazed short by wandering flocks of goats and sheep, all of which had moved on to fresher pastures. The flat lands stretched away from them in every direction, like a giant playing field on the top of the world. The only sound, apart from the chattering voices of the three small boys, was the cawing of rooks as they settled into a spinney of trees for the approaching evening.

The boys walked and ran, pushed and chased one another, laughing with the sheer joy of being alive; even Iqbal finally relaxed. Living amongst the cities, villages and roadsides meant constantly having to be alert, dodging traffic and predators who were always on the look-out for opportunities to make a few rupees or score some food. Out here there were no dangers or responsibilities, they could just be children for a while.

When they finally arrived at Amanat's house his wife was waiting for them. She and Amanat had nine children, including Liaqat, and the tiny compound seemed to be as full of people as the house Iqbal had left a couple of hours earlier. There was a lot of activity around the fire that was burning in the corner of the courtyard and a large pot of rice was steaming as Liaqat's grandmother stirred it at the same time as shooing away the hungry children who were willing to dip their fingers into the boiling water just for a taste.

'Your father's out watering the fields,' Liaqat's mother told him. 'Now you're finally home you can take his meal out to him.'

She handed him the bowl of rice and curried meat, which smelled good and brought the children over from the cauldron of rice to try their luck with the curry. They were immediately sent packing, told to wait their turn.

'Come on,' Liaqat called to his two friends, both of whom had been hoping they'd get to eat themselves before they were sent back out again, 'we'll take the bicycle. That way we'll get back before these locusts have eaten everything.'

Passing Iqbal the bowl of food he pulled the bike out from under a makeshift wooden shelter and climbed on. As Liaqat stood on the pedals Iqbal jumped onto the handlebars, still balancing the bowl and breathing in the aroma of the curry, and Faryad swung his leg over the saddle, his arms round Liaqat's waist. The bicycle wobbled for a moment and Liaqat's mother shouted at Iqbal not to spill the precious food. He stared at it hard as if willing his hands not to shake and spill a drop of his precious cargo. As Liaqat gained speed on the pedals their progress became steadier and Iqbal breathed more easily, screwing up his eyes against the breeze and the glare of the setting sun as his cousin pumped the pedals.

'There he is,' Iqbal shouted after a few minutes, pointing to a tiny figure on the horizon, silhouetted by the sunset, 'over there.'

The ground was so flat and Liaqat's legs so strong from a lifetime of running, walking and pedalling, that the specks on the horizon grew larger every few minutes. Amanat wasn't the only one out watering his land, there were others dotted around the area. In all, Amanat had eight acres, which he leased from a local factory owner. The rent was high and the fields produced only a small return, but it was something and it was better than spending his days sitting at the side of a road trying to sell cups of tea. If you can't read or write there's little you can do to protect yourself when it comes to signing contracts and making agreements with those who can. If he hadn't taken the land on whatever terms the owner dictated there were plenty of others waiting in line behind him who would.

The boys were laughing so much, and calling out to Amanat to tell him that his meal was on its way, that for a moment they didn't notice the man coming out of the trees. When they saw him they were taken by surprise and fell silent, embarrassed to find themselves so unexpectedly close to a stranger. Amanat was still too far away to be able to make out the words they'd been shouting at him, but he guessed and stopped his work to wait for them, suddenly aware of just how hungry and thirsty his labours had made him. From where he was he couldn't see the man in the trees and he wondered, as he wiped his brow and watched, why the boys had stopped when they were so close to the end of the journey.

For a few moments the boys thought the stranger was teasing them when he raised the shotgun to his shoulder and pointed it at them. They thought he was just trying to frighten them off. Maybe he was angry they'd disturbed the peace of his evening, or maybe he was the owner of the land and thought they were trespassing. But he didn't say anything and his silence was unsettling. Fear had only just taken root in their minds when he pulled the trigger. The explosion sounded more like a bomb than a gun. It rolled out across the open land, sending a cloud of startled rooks up into the sky, their angry cawing mingling with the dying echoes of the gunshot.

Chapter Two

A Valuable Boy

Three years before the gunshot that was to change everything, Iqbal was a slave and had been for many years, ever since his half-brother, Aslam, decided it was time he got married.

Aslam was tired of having to find his own meals, mostly by scrounging off his mother or his stepmother, Inayat. He wanted to be able to come home from a day's work at the brick kilns or in the fields and find the cooking pot already on the fire and the bread in the oven. He also wanted to be comforted at night in a way he'd heard other men were comforted.

To get married required money, because what self-respecting father would allow his daughter to be given to a man who never even bought her a piece of gold jewellery? It was unthinkable.

If he wasn't able to afford a few gifts he would never be able to get an attractive woman, one that would be young enough to bear him the children he would need to look after him in his old age. There were always women who needed husbands because their own had died or left them, or because they hadn't been able to capture anyone's heart. But if they were too desperate then they weren't worth having. They were either too old, too lazy, too shrill or too ugly. It was a problem that was taking up all of Aslam's thoughts and the sooner he sorted it out the sooner he would be able to rest peacefully again.

He'd found a girl who he thought would be willing to be his wife, but her father was suspicious and wanted some reassurance that his intentions were good. No father wanted to think that his daughter was going to marry a man who would work her like a slave and give her nothing in return. There would be no honour for the family in such a marriage, just whispered criticisms and knowing looks from relatives.

Aslam had gone to see his father, Saif, with little hope that he would be able to do anything. If Saif had been like other fathers he would have seen it as a point of honour that he helped his son to impress his future in-laws. But Saif was not like other fathers. He had ranted and raved and pretended not to understand what it was Aslam was asking for. He had wagged his finger and warned him that marrying a woman would only bring him heartbreak. He should know, he said, because he'd been married twice and both women had thrown him out. The girl he was living with now, who was also his stepdaughter, kept her head covered and her face turned towards the pot she was stirring as Saif lectured his son on the iniquities of a fate that had burdened him with so many children that he had been left penniless. Like everyone else in the area, Aslam knew it was actually the money his father spent on drugs that had rendered him penniless, but he knew better than to bring up such a topic.

As he left the house empty-handed, Aslam realised he was going to have to find a way to raise the money himself. If only he had something to sell, something of value. That was the moment when he remembered his two half-brothers, Patras and Iqbal, Inayat's sons.

Iqbal was four at the time, although small for his age, and Patras a couple of years older. Aslam had been the same age when his father first arranged for him to work at the brick kilns and he couldn't see why his brothers shouldn't be made to work for the good of the family, just as he had. It was, after all, the family honour that was at stake here.

He went to look for them the following evening, having spent the day talking to some local employers, and he found them playing with a group of their friends underneath the trees beside the canal. The old man who dragged the little Ferris wheel around town behind his bicycle, had set it up nearby and the children were crowding round begging for rides as he laboriously pedalled to turn it. He'd started the evening asking for a decent price for each ride, but had now reached the stage of accepting anything they would be willing to give him.

'You two,' Aslam shouted at his half-brothers, 'I need to talk to you. I have a message from our father.'

Patras and Iqbal trotted over to him. Patras looked wary; having known Aslam longer he realised that he only ever bothered with his half-brothers when he wanted something. Iqbal's eyes were wide with curiosity, anxious to hear what words of wisdom his absent father might have sent across town for him and pleased to receive attention from his big half-brother.

'It's time for you two to work for the honour of the family,' Aslam told them.

Patras now looked openly suspicious, but Iqbal was nodding his agreement. He liked that idea. It sounded important and grown-up. It would be interesting to be allowed a glimpse into the adult world of work.

'Why should we do anything just because you say so?' Patras asked, knowing he was risking a slap.

'Because it's our father's wish,' Aslam said, twisting Patras's ear as he spoke to make sure his words were being taken in. 'I need to take a wife and that costs money. One day it will be your turn and you will understand.'

'How are you going to make us?' Patras said the moment he'd broken free and moved back a few feet.

'I can't make you,' Aslam shrugged. 'But if you refuse to do the honourable thing then Iqbal and Sobya will have to take over your obligations and I would be surprised if even you could live with that shame.'

'But Sobya is just a baby!' Patras protested, horrified at the thought of their little sister being forced to work when it seemed like only yesterday she'd learned to walk.

'Look,' Aslam said, trying to curb his exasperation, 'Iqbal isn't making a fuss. He's more of a man than you and he's only four.'

'We should go to work before Sobya,' Iqbal agreed, ignoring the threatening look Patras was giving him.

'Good,' Aslam said, patting Iqbal on the head. 'That's settled. I've had a word with a friend and he's willing to take you on.'

After that day there was always a great deal of confusion in the family whenever anyone talked about the money that was paid for the two boys, but it was generally agreed that it was a fair sum, a large sum, so large that it would take many years of labour before it was paid off. In reality it was undoubtedly a very small sum, which inevitably grew, as these sorts of debts always do amongst the poor. When an uneducated man is as desperate for money as Aslam was, dreaming of winning himself a beautiful wife, a lender can get away with almost any terms.

Iqbal never truly understood how much he had been worth, but the transaction itself didn't seem strange to him; it was just the way things were done and, as a child, he accepted that. Whenever he did ask questions everyone told him a different story anyway. His mother said the loan was to pay for his brother's wedding, but his new master said it was because Saif was a 'lousy drug addict' and needed to feed his habit. Iqbal didn't like to hear anyone talk about his father in such a derogatory tone, but he didn't argue, partly because he had no idea whether what the man was saying was true or not. He did know that Saif behaved very strangely sometimes, but then so did many other grown-ups in his experience. Knowing, as he did, that asking too many questions tended to anger adults, he kept quiet and just did as he was told.

The master had little respect for any of the parents who supplied him with his labour. He barely gave them any thought at all, unless they tried to cross him or made some petty complaint about the welfare of their children. It was ingratitude he despised more than anything. If he wasn't so generous with his money, how would these people survive at all? None of them were capable of earning the money they needed to bring up their children properly. If it wasn't for him and the money he gave them they'd all be starving to death.

Iqbal had heard the man expressing these views and had no reason to doubt them. He knew how hard it was to earn money and he was grateful to be given the opportunity. From the first day he was taken away, going to work with the master in the early hours of every morning and returning late at night became the normal thing to do. His job at the factory was to crouch in front of a loom and work the threads in and out as fast and as accurately as his little fingers could manage. He was to create the rich patterns that made the finished carpets so desirable, pulling the knots so tight that they would never come undone, no matter how many years the carpets might serve on the customers' floors.

After his first day at work he saw his mother looking sadly at the cuts and blisters on his hands where the repeated movements had worn his skin. He thought he saw a tear forming in the corner of her eye.

'It's all right,' he assured her. 'The master says the skin on my hands will soon grow tougher and it will stop hurting.'

'I wish you didn't have to work so young,' Inayat said, 'but what else can I do for you? If only I had a decent husband and hadn't been left with so many mouths to feed.'

'It's all right, Mama' he told her. 'I understand.'

The man who had agreed to buy Patras and Iqbal wasn't such a bad man; he was just trying to make a living, like everyone else in the area. He wasn't cruel to his workers. He willingly turned a blind eye when the children sometimes giggled because one of them had farted loudly, and was even willing to let them have breaks for meals and drinks, as long as they went back to work afterwards and produced the agreed amount of carpets. He knew that other factory owners managed to get longer hours out of their workers and gave them less food, but he wasn't sure if they did any better in the long run. When he was sitting with friends in the evening, talking about the difficulties of running a business, the others would mock him for being a fool and allowing his workers to take advantage of his good nature. But he believed that if he treated them with some kindness they would repay him with loyalty.

Iqbal was one of his most willing workers, even if he was the smallest there, and the master couldn't help but treat him as a favourite. There was something so charming about those big, serious brown eyes when they looked up, and the boy smiled much more readily and more often than his fellow workers.

'That was my mistake,' the master would tell his friends in coming weeks. 'You should never let them know that you like them, or else they start to take liberties.'

Iqbal hadn't thought he was taking liberties, he just couldn't understand why all the other children were willing to be so frightened of the master simply because he shouted at them sometimes and threatened them. He was so used to hearing raised voices around the house that he didn't find it as intimidating as the others; in fact, he didn't take much notice.

It didn't seem right that they should all work until their fingers bled and their backs ached, so sometimes he would decide he'd done enough for the day and would walk out of the premises, without waiting to be dismissed. The other children would watch with open mouths, unable to believe what they were seeing. How could anyone so small be so brave?

It didn't seem brave to Iqbal, it just seemed like the obvious thing to do.

'Where's he gone?' the carpet master would ask, incredulous to see Iqbal's place empty yet again, and none of the others would dare to answer.

'Where is your brother, Patras?' the man would try again.

'I don't know, Master,' Patras would reply, half angry with his little brother for drawing so much attention to himself and half ashamed that he didn't have the courage to do the same.

The first few times it happened the carpet master went to find Iqbal and explained patiently to the boy that he couldn't leave his workplace without permission. Iqbal listened politely and nodded as if he understood, but he still continued to do as he wanted, making the other children giggle nervously and leaving his owner perplexed. He certainly didn't want to beat such a small boy, but how else was he going to teach him the rules? If he allowed him to continue to come and go as he pleased, it would not be long before the others felt they could do the same, and then where would he be?

After Iqbal had been working at the factory for a few weeks, the carpet master took his complaint to Aslam, telling him that he wanted his money back because Iqbal was not as good a worker as he had seemed at first.

'Just punish him when he's naughty,' Aslam said, unnerved at the thought of having to refund money that he had now spent on gold jewellery for his new bride. To have to sell it in order to refund the carpet master would have resulted in too great a loss of face in the eyes of his in-laws. 'He'll soon learn the right way to behave.'

'But I can't punish him,' the man said. 'He's so small and he looks at me with those eyes …'

'Can't you sell him on to one of your friends?' Aslam suggested. 'Someone who doesn't have such a soft heart.'

The man looked at him thoughtfully and then nodded. That seemed the best way forward. The boy would fetch a good price because his work was of such a high standard. They wouldn't find out what a headstrong spirit he had until too late. He might even be able to turn a profit on the deal.

'All right,' he said with a sigh. 'I will do this favour for you, but if I am not able to find a buyer you will have to give me my money back.'

The next day Iqbal was puzzled, and pleased, by all the attention he received. The master was even nicer to him that usual, bringing all sorts of people over to show them his work. He swelled with pride as the master praised the speed of his fingers and the accuracy of his knots, and he worked even harder and faster under the admiring gaze of the visitors, wanting to show off his skills. The faster he worked, the broader his employer's smile grew. One man seemed to be particularly interested in what he was seeing. He and the master spent a lot of time talking in low voices over cups of coffee in the courtyard outside, and later in the day the man returned.

'Iqbal,' the master said, putting a fatherly hand on the boy's shoulder, 'this is your new owner.'

'I don't understand.' Iqbal looked anxiously across at Patras, who seemed to be equally surprised by the news. 'I'm here with my brother.'

'Your work is so good,' the master beamed, 'my friend here has asked that I allow him to purchase your debt, so you can work for him. It's a great honour.'

Iqbal didn't like the way the other man failed to smile. He was a big man, fat, with mean little eyes. He kept patting at his sweating brow with a rag that he'd rolled into a wad in the palm of his hand. He seemed uninterested in talking to Iqbal, simply wanting to get on his way as quickly as possible now that the deal was done.

'You go with him now and he'll show you where you'll be working from now on,' his old master said.

'Can Patras come too?' Iqbal asked.

His new master clicked his teeth in annoyance at the delay.

'No, Patras is going to stay here,' the old master said. 'Run along now, and work hard for my friend.'

Iqbal stared back over his shoulder at Patras as the men hurried him out the door, but his brother could do nothing but stare helplessly back. This was grown-up business and Patras didn't know what to do. He hoped he wouldn't be in trouble with his mother when he got home for not taking care of his little brother.

The new master didn't speak to Iqbal as he marched to the new place of work, nor did he adjust the length of his stride to take into account the boy's shorter legs. Iqbal had to almost run in his attempts to keep up. When he stumbled on a rock, stubbing his toe painfully, the master stopped and swore, grabbed the boy's wrist and pulled him along faster, anxious to get him to work. He'd been impressed by Iqbal's dexterity and he wanted to get as many hours as possible out of him in what was left of the day.

When they walked into the factory Iqbal was shocked by the expressions on the faces of the other children. They didn't just look like they were concentrating on their work, they looked as if they were frightened to even glance in his direction. The air around them was hot and thick with dust. It stuck to the inside of his throat, making him cough.

His new master gestured to an empty workplace and told him to get on with it. Iqbal sat down and looked around, trying to catch the eyes of the other children working near him, but none of them lifted their gaze from their busy fingers. He wished Patras was there so there would be at least one friendly face. Iqbal didn't realise the master was coming up behind him until a stick hit him across the shoulders, knocking him sideways into a fellow worker. The other child struggled to get back to work as quickly as possible, pushing Iqbal off him. The boy was careful to keep his eyes fixed on his loom, obviously terrified that the next blow would land on him.

'When you work, you don't look around,' the master snarled at Iqbal. 'That's the rule. I've paid good money for you; all you have to do is earn it. If you do your work well you'll be well looked after.'

Iqbal took his lead from the other children, and didn't stop working or move his eyes for the rest of the day. It was hard to do good work because his fingers wouldn't stop trembling. It seemed it was going to take him some time to win over this new owner. He decided to start by showing him what a good worker he was. Then he would explain to him why it was a bad idea to treat people so unkindly.

Within hours his hands were covered in painful blisters and cuts, and he was struggling to stop himself from coughing from the dust. Some of the other children wore pieces of cloth over their noses and mouths to keep the dust out, but Iqbal didn't dare stop work and try to find a piece for himself. Instead, he took shallow breaths through barely parted lips. He felt like crying but desperately held back the tears, knowing that they would just result in blows. By the time he got home and crawled into bed that night every part of him ached. He didn't have the energy to raise the sobs he had been longing to release for hours.

Iqbal gradually grew accustomed to the dust, but he still had difficulty reining in his curiosity – even though he now knew it was a punishable offence to allow his eyes to stray from his knots. Over the following weeks he was continually being beaten when the overseers, who enforced the laws of the master, caught his gaze flickering around the gloomy furnace of the room, but he still had trouble controlling himself.

He knew from the first afternoon that he couldn't hope to walk out when he felt he'd done enough, as he had in the previous factory. This change in his circumstances didn't seem right. It left him puzzled and sometimes even angry, an emotion he wasn't used to. He found his mind wandering back to Muridke as he worked, imagining his old friends playing in the cool waters of the canal, or sitting in the shade with drinks, talking and laughing and teasing passers-by. He wondered why his mother allowed her son to work in such a terrible place. Once or twice he tried to tell her just how bad it was. He had expected her to have a word with the master for him, but she waved away his complaints impatiently.

'Do you think my life is any easier,' she asked him, 'looking after all of you? We all have to work till we die. It's the way things are.'

The two overseers were stupid men and punished him

partly because they'd been told to do so and partly because they enjoyed exercising their meagre allocation of power. But if they had wanted to ensure they'd broken the spirits of their workforce, then beating them for looking around was a viciously effective way of doing it.

From the moment he arrived, Iqbal seemed to be a particular source of irritation to them. The way his eyes darted around the room at every opportunity was all the proof they needed that, however obedient his words and actions might seem to be, his spirit was unbroken and he was still watching for an opportunity to escape. If it hadn't been that he was such a productive worker they would have beaten him to death within weeks of his arrival, but he was a valuable asset and the overseers knew that losing him would have brought the master's wrath down on their own heads.

Both of them had started as loom workers for the master, just like Iqbal. They'd taken the beatings and survived. They'd eventually been rewarded by being allowed to leave the looms, straighten their backs as best they could and terrorise the other younger workers. They saw no reason not to pass their own years of suffering on now they'd been given the authority and heavy sticks to do so. The years of mistreatment they'd suffered themselves might have left their faces gaunt and their bodies bent, but their muscles were as strong as wire and their souls had been hardened with years of suppressed anger.

The children all knew there was never any point in appealing to their better natures or begging for mercy. The trick for avoiding beatings was simply to keep working and never make eye contact, which was exactly why the master had given the overseers the jobs in the first place.

Within a few months Iqbal couldn't remember a time when he hadn't spent virtually all his waking hours in that one room, working all the time. When Aslam had first told him he was going to be working, the words hadn't meant anything to him beyond a promise of an interesting experience. He hadn't been able to conjure up any pictures of what it would be like, beyond the odd loom that he'd seen being worked in the village houses. Life was hard anyway, he'd reasoned. Going to a factory each day to work on carpets didn't seem such a bad way to pass the time, especially if it gave him a skill he would be able to use to earn a living later in life. He didn't want to end up like his father, just sitting around all day, shaking and shouting at people as if his head were full of demons. These were the thoughts he'd had just a few months before.

Now he was unable to remember what it must have felt like to be able to run freely around the village all day, talking and laughing with his friends, lying in the shade when he was tired, searching out something to eat and drink when he was hungry or thirsty.

In the moments when the carpet master was being

pleasant, like when customers or other strangers came to the factory to visit, he would remind Iqbal what a glowing future lay ahead of him if he continued to work so hard and produce such beautiful carpets.

'You see the scars on your hands?' the master had asked one day, and Iqbal had dutifully looked down at his small, dry, cracked fingers. 'They will be your fortune one day. You will thank me for the skills I've taught you here.'

Iqbal would beam proudly at moments like that, despite being nervous that the master's smiles could turn to shouts and blows with no warning, but they were very infrequent. Most of the time the master didn't talk to the workers at all, just hit their heads in passing or screamed abuse at them when they made mistakes, telling them how much they'd added to their debts to him with their clumsiness and stupidity, accusing them of letting him down and trying to ruin him.

Fearful of the consequences, the children very rarely made mistakes. Now and then one of them would cut their fingers too severely on the sharp tools they had to work with to continue and there would be a great deal of screaming from the overseers in case any of the blood dripped onto the valuable carpets. They would have to dip the wounds into burning hot oil to seal them and then go back to work the moment the blood had stopped flowing. Any working time lost would have to be made up that night, and their debts would grow yet again.

Although he hadn't really understood what Aslam had said about having to borrow money to pay for a wedding, Iqbal learned from listening to the elders in the family talking around him while he went to sleep that the master now owned the debt and it was his responsibility to work to pay it off. But the amount never seemed to get any smaller, in fact it increased because of all the fines that had been imposed for slow or bad work, plus the fees levied for the meagre rations of rice and water they were given to keep their strength up enough to stay awake and working.

In the early months at the second factory Iqbal lived his life with a terrible sadness in his heart. He never cried, because that would have brought painful consequences, and so eventually the sadness hardened and dried up inside him. After that the overwhelming sensation was one of heavy exhaustion. It weighed down his limbs and made his head and eyes ache from the moment he woke to the moment he slept. It blocked out almost everything else, forcing him to use every ounce of energy he could muster just to do the jobs he was ordered to do and avoid getting beaten.

Sometimes, while being transported to and from the factory, he would see children running in the streets, laughing and playing games and he would marvel at how they found the strength to move so fast and exude such joy. He could no longer remember ever feeling that strong or that carefree. Just putting one foot in front of the other as he walked from the master's van to the loom and back again at the end

32

of the day was as much as he could manage.

He would seldom be allowed home before nine at night and he would fall fast asleep the moment he sat down on the bed. He didn't even have the strength to ask his mother for enough food to subdue the hunger that permanently nagged in his stomach. Many nights, when he was delivered back, the carpet master would take him to the door of the house so he could personally inform Iqbal's mother how bad he had been, how he had slacked and not fulfilled his quotas of work. Iqbal didn't have the energy to protest when the man asked his mother to discipline him and make sure he tried harder the next day. Once the man had gone his mother would go on and on at him to try harder, slapping him in her frustration. He hated the fact that she thought he was letting the family down, but her slaps didn't hurt compared to the ones he received during the days; he just wished she would believe in him. Sobya would watch with wide, sad eyes, until her mother scolded her for staring and sent her scurrying away on some errand or other.

Each night Sobya would make him a cup of tea and bring it to him where he lay. He would struggle to stay awake long enough to thank her, but usually he was unable to fight off the exhaustion and she would just set it down beside his sleeping head and it would still be there when the overseers woke him in the dark.

CHAPTER THREE

THE POLICE COMPOUND

At four every morning they would arrive at the house and pull Iqbal from his bed. His family had grown so used to the disturbance of their nights that many of them didn't even stir as he was taken from amongst them and forced to walk at an adult pace to the waiting van, his eyes barely open, his joints aching.

He knew he was lucky to at least be able to sleep at home, since some of his fellow workers had to curl up in the pits beneath the looms for a few hours each night, their homes being too far away.

Occasionally the children would have whispered conversations when the overseers were outside and the doors were firmly bolted, and some of the others would tell him of trips that had taken days of driving to get them there. These children had no idea how they would ever get back to their homes or how their families would ever be able to find them. Some of them didn't even know the names of their villages or their areas; the single room of the factory was the only world they knew. Just as he'd been sold by one master to another, they had all been passed from place to place, ever larger sums of money changing hands along the journey, until they ended up there, burdened down with debt.

It was hard to make friends with any of them; they were all too afraid to show their feelings and none of them showed any interest in anything other than themselves. Fear had made them numb to pain, boredom and sadness. Every moment of the day was taken up with trying to avoid being beaten or tortured in some way; it left them with no room for anything else. The best they could hope was to survive to the end of each day.

Sometimes, if the master didn't think Iqbal had worked hard enough during the day, he would be made to work through the night. Not that it made much difference whether it was night or day inside the factory – the light was always shut out. The only thing that occasionally changed was the temperature. The shuttered windows may have kept out the light, but the heat would build up through the walls like an oven; only in the coldest months of the year did the temperatures fall at night to a comfortable level.

There was constant pain in Iqbal's joints from having to crouch in one position all the time, but he'd grown so used to it he was hardly even aware of it any more. Whenever he was allowed to take an hour or so off because visitors had come to the factory and he was able to move his limbs around, it caused new pains in unexpected places, so it was sometimes better to stay locked into the hunched position that his body was used to, avoiding the pain in the same way as he avoided the blows from the overseers. On the rare occasions when he passed his old friends in the village on his way to or from work, he noticed how they were all growing taller. He wondered why he wasn't getting bigger too.

Because he did at least get to leave the factory most nights, Iqbal was able to report back to the other factory children that there was more to the world than the four walls they existed within. When he could be sure the overseers were not around, he was able to assure them, in a hoarse whisper, that not everyone had to work up to eighteen hours a day for no pay; that most people were free.

The others stared at him with open mouths and wide eyes, but he could see they didn't really grasp what he was saying. Working in the gloom for so many years had stunted their imaginations and destroyed any hopes they might have had for being happy. They simply did not see any possibility of changing their lives. Iqbal was unsure what other choices he might have, but he was sure he didn't want to spend the rest of his childhood locked in that room.

'I would be too frightened to be on my own outside,' one of the girls had whispered to him once, and he guessed many of the others felt the same.

Iqbal could understand that fear but, for him, the fear of being trapped inside the factory until it was too late to do anything else with his life was much greater.

Sometimes one of his fellow workers would simply give up the will to live. The last of their strength would seem to drain away from them until eventually they did not respond to the blows from the overseers' sticks and their bodies would be carried away like tiny bales of wool, their empty place taken the next day by a new recruit.

It didn't seem fair to him that any child should have to exist like a caged animal, with no one caring if they lived or died. On the way to and from the factory he sometimes glimpsed other people going about their business, laughing and talking to whoever they chose. He saw people eating when they were hungry and sleeping when they were tired. Surely he and his fellow workers had the same rights to those freedoms as anyone else? It didn't seem right that other people could force them into doing what they didn't want to do. Once or twice he had spoken up in defence of one of his fellow workers, and had been kicked in the back for his impertinence.

On one occasion he had even threatened to go to the police for help, after which the overseers had beaten all the children, so he never dared to say such a thing again. His brain, however, never stopped going over the possibilities of escaping. In his dreams he took all his co-workers with him, running to the safety of the nearest police station.

The older he grew the more determined Iqbal became to make a break for freedom. He was sure it was wrong that the overseers beat their charges so often, gave them hardly anything to eat and drink, and sometimes even took them out of the room and tortured them in ways none of them ever talked about when they eventually staggered back to their work places. However much Iqbal was suffering at their hands, he knew the others suffered worse under the overseers' cruelty. Perhaps this was because they knew he was going home to his family each night and severe beatings would be noticed. Or perhaps it was because there was something in his demeanour that told them he couldn't always be relied upon to play the victim. Most likely it was just that he was the most skilled of the workers, a valuable asset.

He was sure that if he could get to a police station and tell them what was going on, how the carpet master and his thugs held them prisoner and treated them so badly, the policemen would come and close the factory down and return everyone to their families. He was sure the authorities would rescue them if they just knew what was happening. In his fourth year of captivity, when he was eight years old, he decided to escape.

The idea festered and spread in his imagination for months as he played out possible ways in which he would achieve his freedom. He knew it was important that he got it right. The worst thing would be to be caught and brought back because then they would not only punish him to teach him, and the others, a lesson, they would also make sure he never got another opportunity. He only had one chance. He had to be sure.

It would have been easier to escape from home one night when the others were all asleep, but then the master would believe the family were hiding him and would take it out on them, demanding his money back. He didn't want that to happen, so he knew he had to do it during the working hours; then the overseers would get the blame.

The plotting and scheming helped to pass the dreary hours of work, keeping his mind alive and allowing him some hope. He played out the possible scenes a thousand times in his head, but each seemed to carry too many risks of capture. The more he thought about it the more he realised there would never be a perfectly safe time. Sooner or later he was going to have to muster all his courage and just do it.

Eventually a day came when the master was out on business and the overseers were obviously in a lazy mood, expecting to have an easy time. This, Iqbal decided, was going to be as good a day to do it as any that was likely to follow.

The clicking of the looms and the wheezing of the children breathing in the dust-filled air were the only sounds inside the factory. The overseers had gone outside to make themselves cups of tea. Iqbal knew there was a chance that they would fall asleep in the shade, believing everything was under control. He could still hear them talking, even though their voices were muffled by the walls.

He kept working, his heart thumping in his bony chest as he strained to hear any sounds from the outside. After he felt sure it had fallen silent, he stood up from his loom. Nearly forty pairs of eyes looked up from their work, shocked to see someone daring to leave their designated place. Some of them appeared curious and others seemed frightened, knowing that the rebellion of one could bring down a fearful retribution on them all. Most showed no emotion at all; they merely watched him because he was the only thing in the room moving, apart from their nimble fingers and the slowly rotating ceiling fan, which was so high that it made no stir in the air down at their level.

Iqbal crept to the door and pressed his ear to it, ignoring the cramp in his legs and back as he straightened himself for the first time in several hours. There were still no sounds of movement outside. All the children's eyes were now on him as he turned the handle, praying they hadn't locked it. They usually only did that if they were going to be away from the compound, getting themselves a meal or visiting their families. It opened a crack. No locks. He stopped and listened again. Still nothing. The shaft of sunlight dazzled him; his eyes were used to straining to see in the dim glow of the bulb that hung above his loom.

As his eyes adjusted he could make out the bare san-
daled foot of one of the guards stretched out and still.
He opened the door another inch – they would certainly
notice if they were awake. If they caught him, he would
tell them he'd been taken ill. It would still get him a
beating and he would just be put back to work, but it
would be less of a beating than if they thought he was
planning to escape.

When the foot didn't move Iqbal poked his head all
the way out of the door. Both the men were asleep, their
cups of tea sitting beside them, flies crawling on the rims.
The main gate to the compound was standing open and
the street outside was deserted. It was important to move
fast. The moment they realised he'd gone they would take
their anger and embarrassment out on the other children;
he had to get back with help as quickly as possible. He
slipped through the door and pulled it shut gently. At
that moment a lorry driver outside the compound let off
a fanfare of horn blasts, making his heart leap. One of the
guards raised his hand and swatted away a fly, but didn't
bother to open his eyes.

Iqbal tiptoed across the dusty courtyard to the gate,
expecting to hear an angry shout at any second. The
moment he stepped into the street he wanted to run as fast
as possible, but knew he would draw attention to himself
if he did. The street was empty, which made him feel
conspicuous, and his heart thumped as he tried to stroll at

a sedate pace towards the nearest corner. He had no idea which direction he should be going in, his only thought was to get as far from the factory as possible.

The adrenaline was pumping through his veins, giving him an energy he hadn't felt for years. Once he'd turned the first corner he sped up, forcing his stiff joints to run. No one seemed to be paying him any attention and his breathing became laboured through exertion rather than fear.

He had no idea where to find a police station. People like his family never had anything to do with authority figures like policemen and he was unsure how they should be approached and spoken to. But he had no one else to turn to, no one else who he imagined would be willing to stand up to the factory owner and his bullies. The picture of the other children still in the factory filled his mind. He must get help for them as fast as he could. He'd seen how hard the guards would beat the workers if they lost their tempers. Sometimes it looked as if they would kill them before they would relent; sometimes he thought they enjoyed it.

When he'd been running for what seemed like hours, and his legs and lungs both felt like they couldn't take him another step, he found a hidden corner behind some shops and sat down to gather his thoughts. None of the streets he'd run through had been familiar to him and he had no idea if he had run towards Muridke or away from it. He didn't want to go home because he knew that would be the first place the carpet master would go looking for him. He also knew his mother would be angry with him for running away and causing trouble. If there was one thing she didn't want it was for her children to bring home their troubles; she had enough of her own to deal with. Images of the other children in the factory kept coming back to him, making him feel sick with the urgency of his mission to find help, and with his inability to think clearly and know what to do.

He realised he was going to have to ask for help to find the police station. When his panting had subsided enough for him to be able to speak coherently he pulled himself back on his feet and started to ask passers-by for directions. Most ignored him, as if his voice had not registered on their consciousness. Some brushed him aside impatiently, and others listened to his request and shrugged. Eventually a teenage boy gave him some directions.

'Be careful not to upset them,' he warned. 'They like to fill their cell with people like you.' He pulled open his shirt to show a pattern of scars. 'They gave me those to remember my time there.'

Iqbal nodded gravely and set off to follow the older boy's directions. It wasn't long before he came to a pair of solid metal gates. They stretched up towards the sky, crowned with a tangle of barbed wire, which continued to run along the top of the high walls on either side. There was no sign to tell him whether or not this was actually a police station. He looked around for some method of opening the gates but could find none, so he knocked on the hot metal sheets. The resulting sound was louder than he'd expected, as if he'd struck a gong. It made him jump back in surprise, afraid the whole town would have heard; he didn't want them to think he was being disrespectful. A voice on the other side demanded to know what he wanted and when he looked up he saw an eye peering at him through a chink in the metal.

'I wish to see your commander,' he said, as grandly as he could manage. 'I have a crime to report.'

The eyeball looked to left and right, as if worried this might be some sort of trick to make him draw back the bolts, whereupon a horde would invade his little fortress. Apparently satisfying himself that the boy was alone, he opened the gate just wide enough for Iqbal to see he had a rifle in his hand, ready for use, and he nodded for the boy to come in.

The moment Iqbal had squeezed past him the man slammed the gate shut once more and locked it, gesturing with his head towards the office where the commander of the station held court. The compound was completely surrounded by walls and the commander's office was next door to the one cell. Iqbal glanced through the bars as he passed and a dozen or so pairs of eyes stared back at him blankly. Most of them seemed to belong to boys not much older than himself. Outside the cell, friends and relatives of the prisoners sat in the full sun, waiting to see the commander and to plead their cases or pay their bribes. In the shade of the veranda outside the office sat the other policemen on duty and the servants who were there to attend to the commander's needs. It seemed more like a relaxed gathering of friends than a place of work as they chatted and smoked and drank the tea that the tea boys brewed for them.

Somewhere between the group of prisoners' relatives and officials of the station, was another group of men waiting to speak to the commander. Iqbal, suddenly uncertain about the wisdom of his mission, tentatively joined this group. His eyes darted from one face to another in the hope of encountering a friendly or encouraging look. No one seemed to see he was there; it was as if he was too small and inferior to impinge on their vision. Iqbal tried to contain himself in a way that would be appropriate and respectful, but pictures of what might be happening back at the factory if the guards had noticed his absence kept surfacing in his mind as the men around him chatted lazily, smoked their cigarettes and sipped their tea. Eventually he couldn't bear the inactivity a moment longer and walked into the commander's office.

It took a few seconds for his eyes to become accustomed to the gloom. By simply taking a few uninvited paces he had instantly become the centre of attention. The men who had been sitting outside the office now crowded round the unglazed windows to see what would happen inside the office next. How would the notoriously ill-tempered commander deal with this young upstart? Would he be thrown straight into the cell for his impudence? Iqbal wanted to blurt out everything he had to say, but sensed it would be rude and might anger the commander. He forced himself to wait politely to be spoken to.

For a few moments the commander continued talking to an officer standing to attention next to his desk, as if he hadn't noticed the solemn little boy's entrance into the room, or the faces now peering in at the window. He was leaning back in his luxurious office chair with his hands cupped behind his head, as if allowing the breeze from the ceiling fan to dry the wet patches beneath the arms of his dark grey-blue uniform.

Everything else about him, from his moustache to his well-shone boots, was trim and as polished as the bare glass top of the executive office desk that he sat behind. The desk and chair were the only signs that anything had changed in the room in fifty years. While Iqbal waited, a servant scurried in to give the immaculate glass another quick dusting. He had obviously never raised his eyes to the higher regions of the walls, where cobwebs looped luxuriantly amongst the brown stains of age and cigarette smoke.

By the time the man had wiped the whole top of the desk, the commander had still not signified that he had seen Iqbal, and so the man carefully took his boss's immaculate beret from a drawer in the desk and began to beat it vigorously, as if to remove years of accumulated dust. He was anxious to maintain a front-row view of whatever was going to happen next.

The commander's curiosity finally overcame him and he turned lazily to look at Iqbal. The whole room fell silent, waiting to hear what a small boy could possibly have to say to a man of such importance.

'Excuse me, sir,' Iqbal began when he realised he'd finally been granted the stage. 'My name is Iqbal Masih and I have been held prisoner in a factory near to here. There are other children being held there too and they are being beaten and starved all the time …' His speech stuttered to a halt beneath the withering gaze of the commander.

'You work in this factory?' the commander enquired, stony-faced.

'Yes, sir.'

'Do you know the name and address of your master?'

Iqbal reeled off the information, which felt as if it were engraved in his own flesh, as the commander jotted the details down on a pad, which he had carefully removed from another drawer of his splendid desk. He then nodded slowly and made a dismissive gesture to indicate that Iqbal should wait outside with everyone else, going back to talking to the officer beside his desk, as if the interruption to their conversation had never occurred.

Iqbal opened his mouth to speak again but the servant, who had now finished his dusting, took him firmly by the arm and led him back outside, showing him to a bench in the full sun. The other men in the shade returned to their drinking and smoking, pretending he wasn't there as the minutes dragged agonisingly past. Iqbal was almost overwhelmed with impatience, knowing that every moment they delayed in going to the rescue of his fellow workers could be fatal. He forced himself to sit quietly, fearful of annoying the policemen and being thrown into the cell, but he was plagued with thoughts of what might be happening at the factory. He strained to hear what was happening inside the office. At one stage he heard the commander shouting down the phone to someone, but he couldn't make out what he was saying.

People bustled in and out of the door at his bidding and eventually the commander strolled out himself, buckling on his gun belt and adjusting his beret to the correct rakish angle. He shouted out some orders and two of the other officers grabbed their rifles and ran to one of the police jeeps being lovingly sponged down by a couple of ragged-looking young men. The officers shooed the cleaners away and climbed in.

The commander beckoned Iqbal to follow him to the car and gestured for him to climb into the back. Iqbal obeyed, as excited to be riding in a car for the first time in his life as he was to think they were going to free his friends and punish the carpet master and his lieutenants for their years of cruelty.

The gates were opened and the commander settled himself comfortably in his seat, leaning his elbow on the open windowsill, his hand holding the roof to steady himself as the driver put his foot to the floor, scattering people and motorbikes around him. Iqbal felt a glow of pride as he looked out of the window, peering down on the same people who'd been looking down at him on his run through the streets. He felt that some of the commander's splendour was rubbing off on him; he felt empowered and able to achieve anything. He wondered why he'd put off escaping for so long, it had all been so easy.

CHAPTER FOUR

THE PUNISHMENT ROOM

Even with his police escort, Iqbal felt a tremor of fear as they drew up outside the gates of the factory. He would have preferred never to have gone back there again, but then what would have happened to his fellow workers? And what about all the other children in the future who might fall into the hands of these people? It was his duty to make sure the police put a stop to the whole business. He wondered how they were going to be able to fit all the children into this one police car; they really should have brought a lorry with them. He didn't say anything though; maybe the commander had other plans. It was certainly going to be a big job for the police to trace all the children's families in order to return them to their homes.

'Wait there,' the commander instructed Iqbal and the man beside him in the back seat, before climbing out, with the driver walking behind him. By the time they'd reached the gate the carpet master had come hurrying out. Iqbal tried to hear what was being said, pleased to see how humble the man was being; all his usual bullying bluster seemed to have vanished at the sight of the commander's clean, pressed uniform, badges and gun belt. The master's head was bowed and his posture submissive as he dabbed the sweat from his face with the rag he always carried.

The two overseers were standing behind him, obviously nervous but curious to hear what was going on, sneaking furtive looks at Iqbal as he sat proudly in the back of the jeep. He was surprised how different they looked now they'd put down the sticks they always carried when swaggering around the factory premises. They didn't look much older or bigger than him. He could imagine now how they could have been working on the looms themselves just a few years before, and how nervous they must be now in case the police arrested them and tortured them, just like they themselves tortured the other children. He knew he should feel sorry for them, but he still wanted to see the police commander be angry with them for all the bad things they'd done. He imagined the master would already have screamed and shouted at them, maybe even beaten them with their own sticks for falling asleep on the job and allowing him to escape.

The commander appeared not to be listening too closely to whatever the carpet master was saying. He looked around him in a distracted manner as the man pulled something out of his trouser pocket and passed it to him. The policeman accepted the gift without appearing to notice it had arrived in his hand and then turned abruptly on his heel and marched back to the jeep, tucking the package into his breast pocket. Iqbal was puzzled by the action. The carpet master and his henchmen took a few steps back inside the gates and seemed to be waiting for something to happen.

'All right,' the commander snapped at the remaining policeman. 'Get him out.'

Before Iqbal had time to take in the reversal of roles and the collapse of his fortunes, he found himself being marched firmly in through the gates and handed to the carpet master, who took a painful grip of his arm to make sure he didn't escape again. From the pressure in those fingers Iqbal knew just how much punishment lay in store for him once the policemen had gone.

The carpet master shouted effusive thanks to the departing backs of the officials and the overseers slammed the factory gates as the jeep engine fired back into life. Iqbal heard the men he'd thought would be his saviours driving away with a screech of tyres, leaving him to his terrible fate. The master's powerful fingers squeezed his arm so tightly he thought it was going to snap. The carpet master hurried towards the buildings, eager to release his fury at being challenged, inconvenienced, humiliated and forced to part unnecessarily with money. The speed of his strides jerked Iqbal off his feet, but the master didn't slow his pace, dragging Iqbal behind him through the dust as if he weighed nothing.

The overseers followed behind grinning foolishly. At that moment they hated Iqbal with a vengeance for making them look stupid. If they hadn't been so stupid they might have realised that their hatred stemmed from jealousy that he'd had the wit and the courage to try to escape when they never had in all the years that they'd laboured on the looms. The idea of being on their own in the outside world terrified them; they had been inside the factory walls for too long, they wouldn't have known how to survive without the master to feed them and tell them what to do. They would never have had the courage to talk to a policeman and they could only dream of riding in a shiny police car. Most of the children who survived their early years of slavery ended up like them, frightened of the world and unable to find any other place in it.

The master didn't go back into the factory but shouted for one of his henchmen to make sure everyone in there kept working. He ordered the other one to follow him into the room that the children all referred to as 'the punishment room'.

The punishment room was actually a windowless cell, used partly as a storeroom and partly for those in control of the compound to take a child whenever they wanted to separate him or her from the other workers. The master threw Iqbal down on the floor and kicked him hard in the stomach and the ribs before Iqbal had a chance to curl himself into a protective ball. The room was unbearably hot, the ceiling fan resting motionless above them as the master continued to kick the boy around the room, the sweat dripping from him with the exertion.

'Tie him up,' he ordered the overseer when he was finally tired of kicking, and the man came forward with a rope that was kept in the room for just this eventuality. He tied Iqbal's wrists together, pulling the knots so tight they cut into his flesh. He then did the same to his ankles, leaving a length of rope free. Iqbal was unable to stop himself from crying out from a mixture of pain and fear, earning himself another kick.

The master, having recovered his breath, stepped forward and lifted Iqbal upside down from the floor while the overseer climbed on top of some sacks of rice in order to reach the ceiling fan with the spare end of the rope. Iqbal made one last attempt to wriggle and kick his way out of their grasp, but the master landed a punch in his stomach that took away his breath, making all other movement impossible while he fought to recover it. The master took Iqbal's weight until the knots were tied and then let go. Iqbal swung by his feet like a pendulum, back and forth above the floor as his torturers went to the door, switching on the fan as they went.

'You'll think twice before you try something like that again,' the master assured him and then slammed the door shut, leaving Iqbal swinging in the dark silence, the blood roaring to his head.

It was impossible for him to tell how long he hung there with the fan labouring to keep him turning. The only control he had was whether to allow his arms, bound at the wrists, to hang down towards the floor or to lift them up and get a firm purchase with his fingers on some part of his clothing in order to rest his shoulder joints. His body was so racked with pain it was easy to forget he was also sick with hunger and thirst. At some stages exhaustion managed to overcome the pain and he would drift into a strange state somewhere between sleep and wakefulness, waking himself with his own delirious mutterings as he talked his body into staying alive.

He tried to remember all the prayers he'd learned in church as a small boy, but only certain phrases seemed to come to him, and then they would repeat, over and over again. Half of his brain was aware of what he was saying and feared he was sounding like his father when he was in the grips of one of the terrible delusions that haunted him so mercilessly. He must hold on to his sanity. He was determined they would not succeed in sending him mad. The streets were full of men who had given up the struggle to hold on to reality and normality; he didn't want to become another one of them.

By the time they came to cut him down the next day he was only half conscious, but they took him straight back into the factory anyway as an example to the others. All the children's eyes remained fixed on their looms as

Iqbal was given a drink of water and a few mouthfuls of rice, before being chained to his loom and left to make what attempts he could at working.

He had no trouble keeping his eyes on his work because he felt ashamed of having let the others down. It had been stupid and arrogant of him to think he could close a factory and free the workforce all on his own, and he didn't want to see any looks of reproach the others might be sending him. He felt a hopeless despair taking root in his heart. If the police were working for the carpet masters too, what chance did someone like him have of ever being free? Who could he possibly turn to for help? He couldn't turn to his mother or his family and now he knew he couldn't turn to the authorities. There was no one he could rely on in the world except himself.

Late that night the master took him back to his home and ranted at his mother about how bad he'd been. Inayat shook her head in shame at the thought that her son had caused his master such trouble. She assured him it wouldn't happen again and that she would make sure Iqbal was ready for work again the next morning. When she had first heard about Iqbal's escape she had been fearful that the man would demand his money back and call the police when he discovered they had nothing to give him. Now she would have to take great care to keep an eye on him whenever he was in the house. As soon as the man had gone Iqbal lay down on his bed and, despite his mother's furious shouting, was instantly asleep. Once Inayat was busy elsewhere, Sobya fetched a basin of water and silently washed the caked blood from her brother's wounds as he slept.

Realising they had a child whose spirit might be harder to crush than most, the factory owner and his helpers made it their business to watch Iqbal more closely than the others from then on. From the moment they picked him up in Muridke before dawn to the moment they delivered him back into the hands of his mother after dusk, they kept a firm grip on him, chaining his ankles to the loom the moment they got to the factory. It was just as he'd feared; he'd had one chance and he had failed. As his strength returned, however, so did his capacity for skilful work and the master was aware that if he kept the boy alive and healthy he would still get good value for money from him. He just needed to be sure he'd broken the child's spirit.

The carpet master didn't see himself as a bad man, but sometimes he despaired at how hard it was to make a living when his workers were lazy and trying to run away, the buyers were forever haggling over the prices and the police were squeezing him for payments. The merchants who came to buy the carpets always looked so prosperous with their western suits, their briefcases and their air-conditioned cars, and yet they would happily haggle over a few dollars. The police commander must be paid at least five times what he earned, yet still he was willing to take money from a poor man's pocket. There were days when the master wondered if he would ever be able to make enough money to live a decent life. On those days he took his frustration out on the workforce, desperate to force a few more hours of work from them, in the hope of finally turning a profit.

'We have to keep our costs down,' the master would tell the children sometimes, when he was feeling in a munificent mood, 'because the customers in America demand it. They make it impossible for us to pay you high wages because they demand cheap carpets. They're the ones we should be angry with, they're the ones keeping us all in poverty.'

Iqbal wondered if that was true. It didn't explain why the master had to be so unkind to them every hour of the day, but it might explain why he had to hire children rather than adult workers. He began to hate the rich Americans who were deliberately keeping him and his fellow workers in poverty, almost as fiercely as he hated his boss and the overseers.

In the months following his escape bid, Iqbal didn't have the strength to do anything other than the work they set him. He didn't even have the strength to raise his eyes and look around at the others. The overseers thought they had finally succeeded in breaking his spirit as he just kept working, silently and skilfully, producing the sort of carpets that people in the West would pay handsome prices for.

Despite appearances, Iqbal's spirit had not been broken, but he had learned some valuable lessons. He now realised it didn't pay to draw attention to yourself and it didn't pay to let people know what you were capable of – it put them on their guard. As his strength and courage returned he was careful to hide them, appearing as much like the other children around him as possible. Over time, the overseers began to be less vigilant, lulled into a false sense of security by Iqbal's apparent lack of interest in the world around him, believing that, like them, he had learned his place in the world. After a year had passed they occasionally forgot to put his chains on when he sat down to work, being eager to get to their tea in the fresh air. Iqbal said nothing, just kept working and biding his time.

The anger he'd been feeling towards the factory owner and the customers who bought the carpets he produced with so much pain, now extended to the police as well. As a small child he'd always been impressed by the sight of the officers in their smart uniforms, especially the ones important enough to have their own cars to drive around in. When other boys had told him to stay away from the police, because they were his enemies not his friends, he'd chosen not to believe them. He'd even fantasised he might be able to wear a uniform like that himself one day. Now he knew the other boys were right, that the policemen's smart uniforms and guns just gave them the ability to bully and hurt people even more effectively than the carpet master. Although he couldn't quite work out why he felt so strongly, it seemed to him they were worse even than the bullies who beat him every day.

Some days, when he felt very low, he would wonder if everyone in the world was corrupt and cruel, but then he would remember his sister, Sobya, and the children he'd played with in the village, and Patras, and the others at their looms. So was it just that the bad people were the ones with the power? And did they hold that power simply because they were willing to hurt people? None of it seemed right to him. He couldn't match any of the things he was discovering with the lessons he'd heard from the village priest during church services all those years ago, when he was a small boy and still free to go to church. Was there a god looking after the meek and mild, suffering the little children to come to him?

As the months dragged past the overseers grew more careless, sometimes leaving the doors open, even though the master would be furious if he found out because insects could get in and damage the valuable wool. One morning a bird flew in through the open door and began fluttering around the ceiling, battering itself against the walls as if hoping to push its way through the bricks. It didn't seem to be able to work out that if it just headed back towards the light it would be able to escape the same way it had come in. The children, momentarily distracted, looked up at the welcome diversion, some even exclaimed and laughed in excitement. The noise brought the overseers in from outside, brandishing their sticks, ready to punish whichever child had dared to disturb their rest. When they saw the bird their anger turned to panic; if droppings landed on the precious wool they would be severely punished for their negligence in leaving the door open.

The bird seemed determined to try to force its way through a small shuttered window, where only a chink of light was visible through a crack in the wood. The window was in the back wall, on the opposite side to the compound and perhaps the bird could feel a faint draft making its way in from the world outside. The overseers spent a few minutes trying to encourage it to fly to the other side of the room where the door stood open for it, but it kept returning to the same place.

'Open the window for the stupid thing,' one of the men told his colleague, pulling over a bench for him to stand on. Both of them were so intent on dealing with the bird they didn't notice Iqbal's eyes, which had strayed from his work and were intently watching their every move.

The shutters, which Iqbal had never seen opened, proved to be stubborn; their hinges were rusted solid, and it took the men several attempts with their sticks to prise them far enough apart to allow the bird an escape route and to allow Iqbal a glimpse of the small opening they'd been guarding for so long. He saw blue sky and heard voices coming up from the street below. After a few more panic-stricken circuits around the room the bird alighted for a second on the sill of the newly opened window before launching itself back to freedom.

The men, suddenly remembering their charges, returned to hitting the children to show their displeasure at being made to look foolish and inept, forcing them all back to work. Iqbal's eyes reverted to the threads beneath his fingers, but not before he noticed that the men did not bother to fasten the shutters quite as tightly as they had been before. In his imagination he could actually feel the breeze making its way through the stale air from this tiny opening of hope, as if trying to lead him out, like the trapped bird.

It would have been impossible to get through the window while the overseers were anywhere in the compound. It would take too long and make too much noise, and the other children might well give him away rather than risk being punished themselves once he'd gone. In his desperation he'd even thought about running away from home in the night, but since his last exploit his mother always made sure he was never alone and the door to the street was locked at night. She was terrified of the repercussions the carpet master would bring down on the family if Iqbal defied him again.

'Why do you always have to be so rebellious?' she kept asking him. 'Why can't you just accept the way things are, like the rest of us?'

She'd heard that Iqbal had got himself on the wrong side of the police and there was no way she wanted them coming to her door. Every village was full of people who told stories about how much it had cost them to get back onto the right side of some policeman or other after being challenged over some imaginary offence. Inayat couldn't afford to get into such a position. People who couldn't afford to pay policemen what they asked for, tended to end up in the cells and nearly always came out nursing broken bones and deep cuts.

That season the carpet master's fortunes finally seemed to turn. He'd managed to find an honest new agent who was able to sell whatever he could give him for top prices in Europe. The man often came to the factory to collect more stock and when he was there the master behaved like he had a visiting prince on the premises. Carpets would be laid out across the courtyard floor for the agent to view and then sit upon as he drank the tea they served him in their one fine china cup and saucer, and nibbled on snacks that the master's wife would serve, holding her scarf modestly across her face and casting her eyes to the floor. All the time the master would be entreating his guest to 'feel the softness of the pile' or to 'drink in the richness of the colours and the detail of the patterns'.

The children looked forward to the man's visits because for as long as they lasted the master and his men would treat them with affection and indulgence – ruffling their hair as they passed, instead of slapping them round the ears, and complimenting them on the quality of their knots, rather than shouting abuse and hitting them with the sharp weaving tools to make their fingers move faster. Their good mood would often last for several hours after the agent had gone, leaving the master with a wad of money and a glow of achievement and well-being.

All the good business the agent was bringing to the factory, however, made it even more necessary for them to increase their levels of production. One of the ways that the master achieved this rise in productivity was to make them work longer hours, which meant Iqbal often had to sleep the night in the factory, just like the others, working until his eyes finally closed with exhaustion and he had to lie down on his bench or in the pit below it. On these nights all the children would work until well past midnight before they finally collapsed, but the overseers could be heard snoring on their beds in the courtyard many hours earlier.

These hours, Iqbal decided, would be the ones to offer him the opportunity he needed to make his final escape. This time, however, he would not make the mistake of going to the police once he was free. He chose a night when the master and overseers had been awake all day and he believed they would sleep soundly once they finally retired. The master was the first to go, issuing dire threats about what would happen to them if they had not met their quota by the time he returned in the morning. The overseers locked the children into the factory and settled themselves down on the beds outside as soon as they were confident their employer had gone for good.

The adrenaline generated by the belief that he might once again be close to freedom kept Iqbal's eyes open and fingers working as the others around him gradually gave up the struggle against fatigue. He felt sick with tiredness, but his senses were alert as he listened to the sounds of their steady breathing and the occasional grunts and shouts as they suffered the nightmares that haunted all of them.

When he was certain he was the only one left awake, he crept over to the bench beneath the window. It was the first time he'd measured himself beside the wall he was hoping to scale and he was disappointed to find that even on the bench he could only just touch the bottom of the shutters with the tips of his fingers. The hinges were far too stiff for him to be able to move them without using his whole strength.

There was another stool that the master sometimes brought out for visiting customers to sit on if they were too old to get down onto the carpets. Iqbal lifted it quietly and placed it on top of the bench. The whole structure rocked unnervingly beneath his unsteady legs but at least he was now at the right height. Holding his breath in his efforts to keep steady, he put as much force as he could into the opening of the shutter, terrified that if it moved too quickly he would be thrown backwards onto the hard floor below.

With a shattering squawk the first rusted hinge gave in to his tugs and the stool swayed sickeningly beneath his feet. He grabbed the shutter to steady himself and several screws popped out of the rotted frame, falling to the floor with a clatter that he was sure would wake every child in the room. Throwing his arms through the opening, so the sill took his weight, he felt the stool flying out from under him and heard it fall with a mighty clatter.

If the others hadn't been woken before they certainly would now, but with any luck they would be too frightened and confused to say anything for some time. If he was going to get out he had to move fast. His arm muscles straining under the weight of his body, he wriggled through the hole, ignoring the pain of the rough brickwork scraping his chest and ripping the worn fabric of his shirt. He had no idea what lay on the other side of the wall, but there was no time to stop and take stock; he had to have faith.

He launched himself into the unknown headfirst, seeming to hang in mid-air, although in reality it couldn't have been more than a second or two before he landed on the hard ground of the street below, knocking the wind from his chest. He could taste dust in his mouth and spat it out before taking in a deep lungful of air.

He lay for a second, wondering if he would ever be able to breathe again, waiting to see if there would be any shouts or movement inside the building or from behind the compound wall, but everything had fallen silent once more. His legs still shaking from the exertion and excitement, he pulled himself to his feet and limped away into the darkness with no idea where he was headed or what he was going to do next.

CHAPTER FIVE

STREET LIFE

Iqbal certainly couldn't go home as his mother would hand him straight back to the carpet master. This realisation brought a feeling of sadness that tightened his chest whenever he thought about it. He felt bad to think his parents would be in trouble for the money the family still owed, which he hadn't been able to work off in six years of hard labour, but he promised himself he would find a way to pay the man back as soon as possible.

Iqbal was never frightened of working hard. If he could just find someone who would be willing to give him work, pay him some money and treat him fairly he was sure he could repay the debt. But he knew that if he didn't make this bid for freedom he would be trapped in that factory, or others like it, until the end of his childhood, by which time he would be unfit to do anything else as a man, never being paid a penny, the alleged debts always mounting.

His biggest fear was that the carpet master would go to Muridke and demand that Sobya took his place at the loom. His little sister was so quiet and obliging she would never put up any resistance, accepting whatever fate her elders planned for her. She was also pretty, and the thought of how the overseers might treat her made him shudder. He had to find a way to protect her, and the rest of the family, as quickly as possible. But he had no idea where to start on such a mission.

He tried to put any thoughts of what might be happening to his fellow workers back at the factory out of his mind. He told himself that once he was sure of his own safety he would try to find a way to save them; he knew he would never be truly free himself until they too had been released.

The important thing now was to get away from the immediate area of the factory before dawn. He guessed that the moment they realised he'd gone, the master would be out in his van, cruising around the streets in search of him. This time he knew that if he was caught no one would do anything to save him from being dragged back to the factory, least of all the police.

He could imagine the scene in some crowded street if the master spotted him, as onlookers stopped to watch the little piece of free theatre being staged for their entertainment. However hard he might fight and however loud he might shout, the sight of a small boy being grabbed and forced to get into a van would elicit only curiosity. People would smile at any courage he might show and sigh knowingly at the problems parents have with their children these days. The master was a man, an adult, and he would have a vehicle, which would indicate he was of some substance. Everyone would assume he was the one in the right against a small, ragged, dirty boy from the lowest class.

Knowing there was no one in the world who would ever come to his rescue made Iqbal feel desperately alone, which was frightening but exhilarating at the same time. There was no one to tell him what to do or what not to do. What happened in his life now was up to him. But there was no time to worry about that yet. It was vital he stayed out of sight until he was far enough away from the factory to be safe.

He broke into a run whenever he could, but his legs, having been bent in front of a loom for so many years, were not used to so much exercise and couldn't do more than a few yards before they forced him to slow down again, sending sudden pains shooting up through his knees and hips. He'd seen how agile other children were when they ran and played in the streets and knew it shouldn't be like this, but he found it hard to imagine how it felt to have a body that didn't ache.

Eventually, as the light began to lift the cover of the night and people emerged from their houses into the streets to begin another day of drudgery, exhaustion caught up with him, weighing him down and making each step an almost unbearable effort. Every atom of his body longed to sleep but without the darkness to hide him he felt vulnerable and conspicuous. He cast his eyes around for somewhere safely hidden from the world, where he could lie down and give in to the exhaustion for a few hours.

When the silhouette of a derelict building emerged in front of the rising sun, he left the road and climbed through one of its empty, illuminated windows. The rubble of collapsed walls and ceilings had created a landscape of small hills inside, which would shield him from the view of any casual passers-by. It didn't look like a place anyone had stepped into for a long time. Digging out a hole amid the bricks and concrete, he curled up into his hard-edged nest, his head resting on his arms, and instantly fell into a deep unconsciousness. As the heat of the day built up, wrapping him like a blanket, his mind and body soaked up the rest like a parched sponge.

He slept so deeply that even if someone had come into the building he would not have been aware of them and they would probably not have noticed him, just seeing a few dry rags lying amongst the debris.

Through the course of the day a number of dogs came across him, sniffing at what they hoped would be a carcass in their continuous search for anything edible. They all wandered off once they realised there was still breath in his body. When he did finally stir, aroused by thirst and hunger, the sun had moved all the way across to the other side of the building and was growing low once more.

Peeping over the top of the hill that had been his bed he could see the street outside was still bustling with day-lit life. He decided that if he just waited a little longer the light would dim again and would provide shadows he could move through in his search for something to eat and drink before he began his onward journey to his still unknown destination. What he really longed to do was go back home to his mother and the people he'd known all his life, but Muridke was the one place he couldn't go to, which left a hole in his heart. He pictured Sobya's solemn little face staring at him and felt the tears welling behind his eyes.

By the time he felt it was safe to venture out of his hiding place his hunger had grown to an urgent desperation. It was making him feel dizzy and unable to think straight. As the heat of the day cooled, more people were coming out of their houses onto the streets to eat. The aromas of cooking were everywhere as stoves heated up and food began to sizzle, filling his mouth with saliva. Everyone was busy cooking, talking, eating, talking, smoking, talking, drinking, talking; no one bothered themselves with a small boy flitting in and out of the shadows like a night insect. They didn't give him a second glance.

For a few moments he was able to pose as a worker at one of the stalls, clearing away rubbish, pushing anything edible that anyone had left into his mouth. As soon as someone spoke to him he moved back into the shadows and on to the next street to a bucket of slops that stood beside a counter, picking out choice pieces and swallowing them without even chewing. He drank like a thirsty animal from another bucket that stood below a dripping tap, scooping the water, still warmed by the sun, in his cupped hands and pouring it into his parched mouth. He was certain he could feel it spreading through his body, reinvigorating him, rehydrating him, making him alive again. Emboldened by his own returning strength he actually snatched one or two pieces of bread while their owners looked the other way, retreating a safe distance before devouring them. He felt guilty about stealing, but only once the pains of hunger had started to subside and the strength had begun to seep back into his aching limbs.

His stomach felt uncomfortably bloated with more food and water than he had ever consumed in such a short time. Ignoring the feeling of nausea, he returned to his walking, eager to put as many more miles as possible between himself and his past, his mood improving with each step, ready for adventure again.

However hard it might be sleeping rough and scrounging food, it felt like heaven to Iqbal now his hunger and thirst had been sated. To be free to go where he chose, sit when he felt like it and sleep when he was tired, made him almost giddy with joy. But better than all that was the freedom to daydream – to let his mind drift as he walked or sat in a corner somewhere, watching the world go by. To be free to think whatever thoughts he wanted and to be able to look around him without being punished was so good that he sometimes forgot where he was and felt guilty for a few seconds for not working, before he realised there was no one to tell him what to do any more. His natural curiosity had been starved for so long it didn't feel like he would ever be able to see and hear enough to satisfy its cravings.

Despite the freedom, life was still not easy over the following days. People didn't always take kindly to him picking up scraps of food they might have had other plans for. Just because they'd discarded it into buckets or piles by the roadside didn't mean they hadn't been intending to feed it to their dogs, their goats or some other livestock. Most days at least one person would shout their protests and run after him, but it was always too hot for them to keep up the chase for long and Iqbal's legs were beginning to ache less the more he walked; he was becoming almost as fast and nimble as other children who lived or played on the streets.

He learned to choose his sleeping places carefully, not wanting to be taken by surprise while he slumbered, knowing that wherever there were people there was a danger of being captured or hurt by someone who could see he was living alone and unprotected. The carpet master was not the only man in the world who used children as slaves. He'd heard stories from fellow-workers who'd been plucked from the street and taken to factories without their families ever knowing where they'd disappeared to. His only protection was his alertness.

One morning, after a night sleeping in a ditch beneath a clump of bushes, which made up a makeshift hedge between a village and open fields, he was woken by the sound of voices much closer to his hiding place than he would have expected. Immediately alert and ready to move on, he peered out through the undergrowth at the bustle of activity going on in the waste ground, which had contained only a couple of sleeping buffaloes when he'd chosen it as his resting place the previous night.

The focus of the activity was a tractor, which had towed a trailer full of people out onto the waste ground. It had come to a stop and the passengers were all busying themselves turning the trailer into some sort of platform. Under the watchful eyes of the buffaloes they were erecting a canopy above it and hanging bed sheets around the sides with words painted on them. Iqbal had no idea what the words said, but he watched anyway to see if he could work out what was going on. Other children had started to gather around the developing scene, some of them talking to the men and women who were preparing the platform, others hanging back, jostling amongst themselves. Iqbal stayed in the bushes; all the children were from the nearby village and knew each other, he didn't want to be the stranger in their midst, not until he was more sure about what was happening.

Whatever they were organising seemed to take forever, requiring endless discussions amongst the growing crowd of people, but eventually it looked as if they were ready and a man with a thick grey moustache drooping luxuriantly round the sides of his mouth, which made him look even more solemn than he actually was, climbed up onto the platform and held up his arms for silence. The sides of his hair were the same silver grey as the moustache, making him seem like a wise elder amongst the others, even though his face was not especially lined. Some of the people closest to him applauded, drawing the attention of the others to the fact that something was about to happen. Now the crowd had grown bigger and all their eyes were on the man on the platform Iqbal felt it was safe to come out of his hiding place in order to obtain a better view.

A makeshift loudspeaker system had been rigged up and made some unpleasant whining noises as a worried-looking young man handed over a microphone to the man with the moustache and played desperately with some knobs, trying to bring the machinery back under control. The crowd fell into a respectful silence as the man with the moustache and the microphone started to speak.

'My name is Ehsan Khan,' he said over the crackle of the static. 'I am the founder of the Bonded Labour Liberation Front. I am here to tell you that bonded labour is illegal in Pakistan. They have passed a law. No one can force your children to work in the factories and the brick kilns ...'

It took a few moments for Iqbal to work out what he was talking about, to realise that he had himself been a 'bonded labourer', a term he was not familiar with. Ehsan Khan was becoming more and more animated as he talked, using words like 'slavery' and 'freedom' and gesturing across the fields to the red chimneys of the distant brick kilns as they drizzled their smoke into the warm morning air. Iqbal had never given any thought to what happened in those strangely shaped places, beyond knowing that his brother, Aslam, and other young men in the village had worked there from time to time. Like everyone else, he'd passed them by and seen figures crouched over the piles of bricks or moving slowly around the bases of the chimneys, as if carrying the weight of the world on their shoulders. It hadn't occurred to him they might be children, just like him, who were being forced to work off debts, beaten and badly treated by their bosses. He moved closer to the platform, screwing up his eyes in concentration as he tried to catch every word that the wise man with the moustache was uttering.

Ehsan Khan painted a terrible picture of the heat and the dust from the furnaces and the years of backbreaking toil the workers were forced to endure, their children having no choice but to follow in their footsteps with no hope of escape. So transfixed was Iqbal by the picture being painted for him in words, that he forgot himself and his own situation. It was only when he realised the man on the platform was talking directly to him that he woke up from his thoughts and found he'd moved into a position where he'd been noticed. His first instinct was to turn and run before anyone grabbed hold of his arm or asked who he was or where he'd come from, but Ehsan Khan's voice was so calm and so reassuring he paused for a moment.

'What's your name, young man?' Eshan asked and Iqbal felt the eyes of the crowd turn onto him.

'Iqbal Masih,' he replied, his legs shaking beneath him. His reply sounded weak and small beside the amplified voice of the speaker. He hadn't talked to anyone for days and the words croaked as they came out. He immediately regretted giving them his name, feeling sure the carpet master would have been asking everyone in the world to keep an eye out for him.

'Do you work in a factory?' Ehsan asked.

'Yes,' he nodded, wondering if it was too late to run now, but not sure his shaking legs would carry him any more. He glanced anxiously around in case there was a policeman listening.

'Don't be afraid,' Ehsan reassured him. 'No one can make you go back if you don't want to.'

Iqbal knew that wasn't true from his own experience with the police commander, but he liked the idea and didn't run.

'Come up here and tell us about your life,' Ehsan beck-oned him, staring straight into his eyes. Ehsan was aware that if he allowed his gaze to wander the boy might disap-pear and he would never be able to find him again. There was something about his face, old before its time, that told Ehsan this was a boy who had experienced terrible things, but there was wisdom in his eyes and Ehsan wanted to find out what he knew. It was obvious from the way he was staying separate from everyone else that he wasn't from the village, and it seemed likely from his ragged appearance that he was living wild for some reason. Ehsan hadn't consciously noted all these points, he'd just seen the little figure watching him intensely and had known there was something special about him.

Iqbal's eyes flashed around the crowd. Everyone was looking at him, which made him want to run, but none of them appeared to be threatening or aggressive; they mostly seemed curious to hear what he might say in response to the man with the microphone. One or two smiled and made encouraging signs with their hands, as if trying to waft him up onto the platform. As he walked forward he was worried his legs were going to give way beneath him. When he reached the edge of the platform, helping hands lifted him up and for a second he was flying before coming to land beside Ehsan Khan.

Ehsan held the microphone close to Iqbal's mouth. 'Tell us about your life,' he said again, coaxing the boy to talk.

The crowd had fallen silent, wanting to hear what he had to say. Iqbal cleared his throat, shocked by how loudly his own noise came back to him through the speakers on the platform.

'My name is Iqbal Masih,' he said again. Something about Ehsan Khan made him feel safe and protected enough to reveal himself. 'I come from Muridke. When I was four years old my mother and father needed to borrow money for my brother's marriage. The owner of the carpet factory lent it to them and I went to his factory each day in order to work to pay off the debt. Then the owner of the factory sold me to a friend of his who had another factory, and that was where I had to stay. I went every day and worked, and sometimes at night too, for years.'

'How old are you now, Iqbal?' Ehsan asked.

'I think I'm ten,' Iqbal replied. 'I'm not sure.'

'So you have been working for six years. You must have paid the debt off by now.'

'No.' Iqbal shook his head, as Ehsan had known he would when he asked the question. The boy's courage was building now that he could feel the crowd were listening to him, wanting to know what he would say next. 'The debt grew bigger because the carpet master had to feed me every day and sometimes I would make mistakes and a piece of work on a carpet would be ruined. The cost had to be added to what I owed.'

There were some noises of disapproval amongst the

crowd; this was a story they'd heard before about other factory and brick kiln owners. Once you owed money to these people the debt could never be paid off, everyone knew that, but no one knew what to do about it. Iqbal felt himself relaxing in front of so many friendly, encouraging faces, actually quite enjoying the attention. He was relieved to see they were shocked by what he was saying and thought it was wrong, because that was what he had always thought. Everyone around him at home and in the factory had gone on as if his situation was the most normal thing in the world. He'd sometimes worried that he might be mad for believing life shouldn't be like that, but the expressions on these people's faces were telling him he was right.

'Was the carpet master kind to you?' Ehsan asked, knowing again what the answer would be.

'No. He often beat us and sometimes he would hang us from the ceiling by our feet if we had done something wrong.'

The crowd let out a collective mutter of horror at the thought and Iqbal looked round at them with a shy smile, pleased to have been able to inspire such a reaction in so many people. He liked the feeling of being up in front of the crowd with all eyes on him and all ears listening to his words; no one had ever listened to him before or encouraged him to voice his thoughts, quite the opposite in fact. From as early as he could remember grown-ups had always been telling him to be quiet and to stop asking so many questions.

'How did you come to be here?' Ehsan asked. 'This is a long way from Muridke.'

Iqbal put his hand over the microphone and spoke quietly to the man beside him, suddenly worried again that he was giving too much away.

'I ran away,' he whispered. 'If they catch me they'll punish me again. I think next time they might even kill me, they will be so angry.'

'You never have to go back there, Iqbal. The government has cancelled all bonded labour debts.'

'But the police are on the side of the carpet master,' Iqbal said, forgetting the crowd as he tried to understand what Ehsan was telling him.

'Not if you're with me,' Ehsan said.

'What about the others in the factory? They're my friends. I want to be able to help them.'

'We can help them,' Ehsan assured him, then turned back to the crowd. 'We can help all these children if we want to!' The crowd cheered and Ehsan went back to Iqbal. 'But first we must get you to somewhere safe, somewhere the carpet master can't reach you.'

The meeting went on for another hour or two and Iqbal sat quietly on the ground beneath the trailer, waiting for Ehsan to be finished with the people who came up to talk to him and to take leaflets about his organisation.

His heart was thumping in his chest and all his limbs were trembling. He remembered how he had trusted the policemen and how they had betrayed him, and now he was trusting someone else who he knew nothing about. But what else could he do? He didn't want to have to keep running and hiding for the rest of his life. On his own he could do nothing to help his fellow workers or protect Sobya, but if this man was true to his word he might be able to offer protection.

There was something about the people on the trailer that excited him, that made him want to be part of whatever it was they were doing, and made him feel safe. They seemed to be so fearless about speaking out against unfairness and they seemed to understand exactly what he had been through, without him having to explain. He'd never met people who seemed to be so free and sure of what was right. They wanted to change things, something that no one in his village would ever dream of suggesting. Iqbal thought of his family and the way they were always willing to accept whatever was told to them or done to them. If he had a father like Ehsan Khan he would never have ended up in a factory. He didn't blame his parents or his brother, but he didn't want to be like them either. He wanted to be like these people. He wanted to be like this man with his funny moustache.

If it was true that all bonded labourers were being held illegally, Iqbal wanted to go into every carpet factory and brick kiln in Pakistan and spread the word as quickly as possible, starting with the children who he'd worked alongside for so many years. He felt a knot of excitement in his stomach at the prospect of leading them out of the factory into the sunshine, but still couldn't dispel the terrible feeling of dread that he was being stupid and would soon find himself being delivered back to the carpet factory, once again at the mercy of his oppressors. What if the carpet master offered Ehsan Khan a bribe, like he had given to the police commander? Would Ehsan be able to resist the temptation when such a senior officer was unable to? Iqbal wanted to believe that he could, that this man could be a hero, but he hardly dared to. Part of him was tempted to slip away unnoticed and to go back to relying on his wits to survive, but another part didn't want to be alone any more. He felt Ehsan and the others might look after him, and that was a feeling worth taking a risk for.

As the meeting came to a close all the people on the platform with Ehsan joined him in a chant, their fists punching the air triumphantly.

'We are free! We are free! We are free!'

Looking up from the ground, Iqbal saw Ehsan beckoning him back onto the platform, smiling encouragingly. Iqbal scrambled to his feet, grinning happily.

'We are free! We are free! We are free!' he joined in the refrain, lifting his arms in the air and feeling a rush of joy unlike anything he'd ever felt before.

Chapter Six

Lahore

Even when the meeting was over the crowd didn't want to let Ehsan Khan go, flocking round him, trying to shake his hand or catch his eye. Everyone had a story to tell him or a favour to ask. One of two people were aggressive and shouted abuse at him, calling him a liar and an enemy of Pakistan, but he met their anger with a forgiving smile and moved on to the next person without responding. Their shouts frightened Iqbal and made him want to run. They reminded him of the carpet master and he guessed they were men who kept bonded labourers or were fathers who had sold their children and didn't like to be criticised for following what seemed to them to be a tradition. He didn't understand what they meant when they said he was an enemy of Pakistan, but he told himself that if Ehsan wasn't worried then he had no need to be either.

Iqbal watched in fascination as the people kept on coming up and shaking his new-found friend by the hand, some of them holding on as if they never wanted to let him go. Many in the crowd were too shy to speak themselves, but hovered on the fringes of the group, just watching, smiling and nodding their approval of all the things that were being said. It seemed so far from the darkness of the carpet factory, where no one smiled unless it was to make a sale to a customer.

The heat of the day had built to an uncomfortable level by the time they finally dismantled the platform and turned it back into a plain farm trailer. Everyone's shirts had become drenched with sweat from their labours at a time of day when most sane people sought shade. The tractor drove away and suddenly it no longer felt like an event, just a bunch of people standing around on a piece of empty land, talking to one another.

Iqbal wished they could go; he'd given out too much information about himself, he realised that now. Someone could be talking to a policeman about him at this very moment, and then they would come and grab him back. His eyes kept flickering around all the entrances to the piece of land, his ears straining for the distant roar of an approaching police vehicle, as he forced himself to wait politely.

'Come, my young friend,' Ehsan said eventually. 'It's time for us to go.'

He led the way to a car, which was waiting by the road. It was an old, battered machine, the survivor of a thousand bumps and scrapes on the overcrowded streets of Lahore, but to Iqbal it looked like the property of a rich man. As he approached the open door he felt a flutter of nerves, remembering how he'd become imprisoned in the police jeep and returned to his owner. He hesitated, tempted to refuse the ride and insist on staying independent. But that would be foolish. They were offering a hand of friendship; if he let them drive away without him what chance was there he would ever find them again? Steeling his courage, he took a deep breath and stepped through the door into the oven-like heat of the interior.

Now the option of running away if danger threatened had gone. He'd surrendered himself to trust. Several other people from the platform were coming with them and by the time everyone was in he found himself crushed in the middle of the backseat between Ehsan and a large woman, who reminded him of his grandmother and who said her name was Mrs Baber. She didn't seem as pleased to have him in the car with them as Ehsan was, and fanned herself vigorously and irritably with her hand as more and more people squeezed in around them.

Eventually they could force no more bodies in and the car wheezed and stuttered its way out of the inadequate patch of shade it had been standing in, bumping over the unmade village road towards the nearest highway, leaving a trail of black smoke from its exhaust.

'Take us to Muridke,' Ehsan instructed the driver.

'No!' Iqbal shouted, struggling to get past Mrs Baber to reach the door, willing to throw himself out of the moving car rather than be returned to his former life.

'Oh, my God!' Mrs Baber wailed, pushing him angrily back into his place. 'You stupid boy, do you want to kill us all?'

'Don't take me back,' he turned to Ehsan. 'I beg you, please don't take me back. Just let me out here, you can forget you ever saw me. If I go back now they'll kill me, just to teach the others a lesson.'

'Quiet, child,' Ehsan said, but his voice was gentler than Mrs Baber's. 'No one is going to send you back. We're going to take you with us to Lahore and get you an education, but we have to let your mother know where you've gone. We can't just kidnap you off the streets. That would make us no better than the factory owners who steal children from their villages.'

'But she'll tell the carpet master where I am,' Iqbal protested, 'and they'll send the police to fetch me back.'

'Lahore is a big place,' Ehsan reassured him. 'They won't find you, and anyway you'll be safe with us. We're used to hiding children from people who believe they own them. Trust me, Iqbal, I will not let any harm come to you.'

Iqbal quietened down, not because he trusted anyone, even this kind-faced, gently spoken man, but because he could see there was nothing he could do about it. He had allowed himself to be lured into yet another trap. Was there no one in the world he could trust? There was no chance of getting away from these people, so if they were going to take him back to the carpet factory and claim their reward, like the policemen, he would just have to accept it and plan another escape later if he survived whatever punishment lay in store for him. His heart was crashing in his ears by the time the car was bumping down the road towards Muridke.

'Where's your mother's house?' Ehsan asked as they parked beside the canal and a group of curious boys gathered around. They'd all heard about Iqbal's escape – there had been angry words exchanged in the alleyway outside Inayat Bibi's house, ugly threats meant for everyone to hear. They stared in open-mouthed fascination as Ehsan and his fellow travellers clambered out of the car, assuming Iqbal was being brought back by the authorities to face the music.

Iqbal avoided all their eyes, not able to find the words to speak to the playmates from his childhood before the factories, when there were so many other thoughts churning through his head. None of them plucked up the courage to speak to him, flanked as he was by city people who just might be policemen out of uniform. Mrs Baber shooed them away from her as if they were tedious puppies nagging her to play. She pulled her scarves around her as if preparing herself to do battle.

'This way,' Iqbal told them, walking towards the alley that led to his family's home. Ehsan and his colleagues walked behind, surrounded by a growing crowd of curious onlookers. There was only room in the alley for them to walk in single file and so the crowd's pace slowed down, but other faces appeared in doorways and on the roofs, watching Iqbal's progress at the head of the procession.

Ehsan nodded greetings to everyone as he went, as if they were all personal friends, and some of them nodded back, unable to keep the looks of puzzlement from their faces. Some of the children were sniggering to one another behind their hands as their courage grew; one had picked up a bunch of twigs and was holding them under his nose in a caricature of Ehsan's moustache. Mrs Baber was tutting at the state of the drains that ran along the sides of the alley, holding her scarf across her face to keep the stench at bay and lifting her skirts clear of the dirty water as she waddled awkwardly along.

'This is my mother's house,' Iqbal announced as they reached a pair of wooden doors set into the alley wall. He wished he had the courage to try running away now, before it was too late, but there were too many people and he knew he would never be allowed out of the village.

Ehsan knocked politely, ignoring the shouts of advice from neighbours. Iqbal was shivering and Ehsan put his arm around the boy's shoulders to comfort him. Iqbal wondered if it was to make sure he didn't run away. There was no sign of movement from inside the doors but after a few minutes a boy came down the alley from the other direction. It looked as if someone had fetched him with the news of the visitors. Iqbal felt his heart lift at the sight of him.

'This is my brother, Patras,' Iqbal told Ehsan. 'He works for a kind man.'

'We're looking for your mother,' Ehsan told the expressionless boy. 'We'd like to talk to her.'

Patras, having been called from his place of work unexpectedly, didn't know what to make of this sudden reappearance of his missing brother amid all these strangers. He made no response but unlocked the wooden doors to allow them in. Iqbal went first and Ehsan followed with Mrs Baber and two other men who had been in the car. Iqbal felt comforted by the dignity that these people around him were exhibiting, but still couldn't understand quite what plans they had for him. He wanted to hug Patras and tell him all about his adventures, but something in his brother's expression made him think such a show of affection would not be welcomed. It was as if being with Ehsan and the others had removed him from his brother's world. He didn't know what to say to him. He went back to worrying about what was going to happen next.

What would they do if his mother demanded they hand him back? What if someone was at this moment running to tell the carpet master that Iqbal was in the village? How would they stand up to threats and violence and bribes? If the overseers arrived brandishing sticks would

Ehsan be able to protect him? He didn't look like the sort of man who would know how to fight, nor did any of his helpers. In fact, Mrs Baber was the most frightening one amongst them.

Once inside the house they sat around on the beds, waiting for his mother to appear. A neighbour's wife, keen to be at the heart of the excitement, made tea for the visitors and ensured they were all comfortable under the warm breeze of the ceiling fan while everyone waited. Ehsan stroked his moustache but showed no other sign of impatience as word spread round Muridke that there were strangers in the village. Every so often he would catch Iqbal's eye and nod, as if to reassure him that it was going to be all right, that he must have faith. Mrs Baber sighed a great deal and mopped at her brow with a handkerchief as more and more neighbours and relatives shuffled into the room to stare at the visitors.

Iqbal's mother made an entrance into the room about twenty minutes later, shouting instructions to her children and other relations as she came, apparently anxious to give the impression she was in charge of the situation, but that she was a busy woman and the visitors awaiting her were not the only thing on her mind. Iqbal felt a strong urge to clamber off the bed and hug her, but she didn't look at him or signify she had seen him, so he remained still and silent.

Ehsan swallowed whatever irritation he might have

been feeling at Inayat's high-handedness and stood up politely as she pushed her way through the tangle of knees that filled the tiny room. He bowed his head respectfully.

'A pleasure to meet you Inayat Bibi,' he said and she nodded her understanding that this might be the case before shooing some of the people on the bed, including Mrs Baber, to one side to make room for herself. Ehsan sat down again. Mrs Baber grumbled softly, the downturn of her mouth demonstrating her considerable distaste for the whole scene.

'I run an organisation called the Bonded Labour Liberation Front,' Ehsan said in as casual a tone as he could manage, 'and I would really like to do something to help your son, Iqbal.'

Inayat's eyes were now fixed on the visitor. Having worked out that he was the senior person in the party, she was interested to hear what would come next, quite unable to think of an appropriate response to his words. If anyone was going to be handing out money, this would be the man.

'I think he's a boy who would benefit greatly from receiving an education,' Ehsan continued. 'We would like to take him to Lahore with us so he can attend one of our schools. It would also be a great benefit to you, would it not, to have a son who can read and write and help the family?'

Inayat did not respond to the question immediately. Her face gave away no emotion as she thought through his words, searching for a way to benefit from what was being offered, wary that these educated people might be trying to take advantage of her, trying to rob her of her most valuable asset.

'We have a debt to the carpet master,' she said eventually. 'We need Iqbal to work to pay it off. If he doesn't do it, his sister will have to take his place.'

'The debt is illegal,' Ehsan said, handing over a leaflet that explained the government's new ruling on bonded labour. 'If the carpet master comes complaining you can show him this. He knows he cannot force you to repay any more money. The work Iqbal has done for him has repaid the loan a thousand times over already. He will understand that, however loudly he may shout to the contrary.'

Inayat stared at the leaflet for a moment, unable to read any of the words. Everyone in the room knew that the carpet master was very unlikely to be at all understanding about losing one of his best slaves but Inayat felt too outnumbered to protest and Ehsan was anxious to get away from Muridke as quickly as possible, before the initial shock of their arrival had worn off and other people started to ask what benefit might be in this new arrangement for them. Like Iqbal, he was not keen for a confrontation with an irate carpet master in these backstreets.

'If you allow Iqbal to come with us, we will be able to send you some money each month,' Ehsan went on. 'But if you allow the carpet masters to take any more of your children that money will stop coming.'

Iqbal looked up in surprise. Was this man really willing to pay his mother to keep Sobya safe? He looked across at his mother and found she was looking at him. To his surprise, tears sprang into her eyes as she opened her arms to hug him.

'You are going to be leaving me and going to the city,' she wailed. 'My favourite son is leaving home.'

None of her other children appeared to react to this surprising denigration of their status. Ehsan stood up, taking this as a cue for them to depart and Mrs Baber followed his lead, forcing her way out into the courtyard, heading for the alley as fast as she could go, unable to disguise her dislike for Inayat a moment longer.

To persuade Inayat to loosen her grip on her son, Ehsan produced some rupees from his pocket and passed her a couple of small denomination notes as a down payment. It pained him to allow himself to be manipulated but he was anxious to get Iqbal away as quickly as possible. He knew it was only a matter of time before the crowd found its courage and started to think of new demands to make. Inayat slid the money into her sari without even acknowledging its existence and released Iqbal from her arms.

As he came out into the courtyard Iqbal saw Sobya hovering in the door to the kitchen. She raised her hand to just above waist height and waved. He waved back. He wanted to go across to talk to her, to assure her he would make sure she was all right, but the movement of the crowd forced him out through the gates.

Once they were back in the alley they had to push their way through the neighbours who had all congregated outside Inayat's doors in the hope of witnessing some drama. The visitors had now been there long enough for news of their arrival to have filtered through to every house in the village. Not much happened in Muridke on a hot afternoon and any sort of diversion was welcome. As they came out into the bright sunlight beside the canal an even larger group had gathered around the car and some of them were shouting angrily. Iqbal recognised the voices as belonging to men who were friends of his father, men who didn't like the idea of change, who found life very comfortable just as it was; men who resented outsiders coming into the village, telling them how they should live their lives and how they should raise their children, doing business with the women behind their backs.

Ehsan, sensing the mood of the crowd was deteriorating, hurried his little party towards the car and ignored the voices. One was louder than the others, ranting nonsensically and he guessed it might be Saif Masih, Iqbal's father, staking his paternal claim. Other men were joining in with whatever he was saying, shouting their agreement. Iqbal was looking around him with wide, nervous eyes, frightened that someone might be about to grab him and take him away from Ehsan before they'd had a chance to escape.

Ehsan pushed him through the open door at the back of the car and he fell against Mrs Baber, who'd got in from the other side. She was shouting back at the crowd of men angrily, telling them they were 'stupid' and 'monsters'. The driver, frightened his car might be overturned into the canal, had started the engine even before Ehsan and the other passengers had managed to pull the doors shut after them.

Fists hammered on the roof like falling rocks and angry, contorted faces ran alongside the windows as they moved off. Turning onto the narrow bridge across the canal, they shook off all but the most furious attackers. By the time they were accelerating up the main road in a cloud of dust, however, the protesters had fallen away and could do nothing but shake their fists and shout abuse at the disappearing car.

Ehsan let out a deep sigh and looked down at Iqbal, who was shivering beside him. 'Don't worry,' he said, 'you're safe now. You don't have to go back there until you feel ready.'

Iqbal nodded but still couldn't stop the shivering. Seeing his mother and brother and sister again in such strained circumstances had left him feeling confused and disorientated. Even though he'd only just met Ehsan, the serious-faced charity worker seemed more like a parent to him that either of his real parents. Thinking of his mother and father as being potential enemies made him feel treacherous and guilty and he wanted to feel differently about them. He wanted to believe they were on his side, not the carpet master's.

'Don't worry,' Ehsan said again, patting his hand. 'One day you'll be able to go back to Muridke with your head high and you'll be able to help your family in ways you've never dreamed of. The most important thing is that you get an education. It's your right. It's the right of every child.'

'Here, boy,' Mrs Baber said, pressing a biscuit into his hand. 'Eat.'

She smiled for the first time since he'd met her, pushing a whole biscuit into her own mouth to show him it would be all right. He realised how hungry he was. He hadn't eaten anything since the previous evening, when he'd managed to wrestle some scraps from a stray dog.

As they drew closer to the city the road became busier. They crossed a bridge, around which birds of prey were swooping down out of the sky, diving into the water for fish. Fruit and berry sellers held out plastic bags of their wares towards the passing cars in the hope that someone would stop and buy, although hardly anyone seemed to. The driver, who'd been hitting his horn every few seconds all the way down the motorway, now began a frenzy of hooting as he swerved and dashed through the dense throng of brightly painted and decorated lorries and motorised rickshaws, all ladened down with passengers. Faces looked in at every window as people weaved in and out of the apparently random streams of traffic each time they ground to a halt in the smoky congestion.

Iqbal felt a mixture of excitement and fear as the noise grew louder and the scene more frantic, but none of the other occupants of the car appeared to have noticed anything. They all called out contradictory directions to the driver to help him find the fastest route through the chaos to their destination and Mrs Baber handed out another round of biscuits. Everyone was sweating profusely as the sun beat down on the roof of the car, and the breeze, which the motorway had afforded them through the open windows, fell away to be replaced by exhaust fumes and a heavy stillness in the air.

Beggars leant through the open windows with their hands out and missing limbs on display, many of them children. One or two of them had meagre wares to sell or made an attempt at cleaning the filth of the journey off the windscreen.

'How old are you?' Mrs Baber would shout at them if they came close enough. 'Why aren't you in school?'

The beggars took no notice of her and now and then

the driver would pass some rupees out to someone who had managed to touch his conscience.

To Iqbal's wide and amazed eyes there seemed no rhyme or reason to anything that went on around them as they turned and twisted down side roads past once grand, now crumbling, buildings, the car nosing through crowds of people and traffic until it eventually came to a halt outside high gates of sheet metal in a backstreet.

'Thank God,' Mrs Baber sighed as they clambered out of the car and stretched their aching limbs, their sweat-drenched clothes clinging to their skins. Ehsan was knocking loudly on the gates as Iqbal looked around, wondering at the tangle of electric and telephone wires that looped amongst the houses. Plant life had taken root in every crack and crevice of the elderly buildings, roofs and walls sprouting shrubs and weeds, contrasting with the dusty, barren earth of the street.

'This is our Freedom Campus, where you'll be staying to begin with,' Ehsan explained as a pair of eyes peered cautiously through a hole in the gate, before drawing back the bolts and pulling them far enough apart to allow the arriving party entry.

Mrs Baber went straight to the tap inside the entrance and splashed cold water on her face, jabbering instructions for tea to a couple of young women who were sitting outside a small kitchen. Ehsan smiled conspiratorially at Iqbal and steered him through to a doorway on the other side of the courtyard. Inside there were a number of rooms, one of them a large, high-ceilinged hall. The walls were painted a dusty pink, making it feel cosy and safe.

There were posters on the walls and he recognised some of the words as being the same as the ones on the bits of paper Ehsan and his colleagues had handed out from the platform. Iqbal squinted at them for several minutes in the hope they would start to make sense to him if he concentrated for long enough, but they refused to speak to him.

A small baby was lying on a mat in the middle of the room under the draft of a ceiling fan, sleeping deeply. Iqbal walked over to the child and stood looking down at it for a few moments, lost in thought, enjoying the breeze from the fan on the back of his neck, feeling it drying his shirt. Everything was moving so fast, he felt confused. Just a few hours ago he'd been living wild under a bush and now he was in the middle of a terrifying city.

It was comforting to watch the steady breathing of the baby as its ribs rose and fell peacefully. He tried to imagine what it must have felt like to be that helpless, before he grew up and had to take responsibility for earning money. He thought it must have been a good time, a time when he could rely on his mother to look after him and protect him. For a fleeting moment he envied the little creature lying on the floor, oblivious to everything going on around it.

When he came out of his reverie and turned round, Ehsan had disappeared and he felt a stab of disquiet, as if he'd been abandoned. He walked quickly back to the door, following the sound of men's voices, which led him to another small room. Inside Ehsan was sitting with two other men round a table. There were more posters on the wall and a large old-fashioned office telephone stood in the middle of the table. The men nodded a greeting to him as he came in, but their faces were serious and unsmiling. He nodded back, feeling grown-up.

'This is Iqbal Masih,' Ehsan told them. 'He spoke to the crowd today and told them what it's like to be a slave. He spoke bravely and made them listen. He'll be a great asset to the cause.'

Iqbal dropped his head and stared at the floor, unsure how he was meant to react to such compliments.

'Lift your chin, Iqbal,' Ehsan said sternly. 'Always walk tall. You're a free man, you must learn to think like one; if you believe you're a slave then you'll still be enslaved. Someone is only a slave if they agree to be one.'

Iqbal lifted his chin and stared hard into Ehsan's serious face. 'I understand,' he said, and for the first time he actually thought that he did.

'Are you hungry?' Ehsan asked.

'Yes, sir.'

'Then let's see if there's anything to eat in the kitchen.'

Ehsan nodded to one of the other men, who scurried out to the courtyard in search of food. Iqbal was impressed by the way people always seemed to do what Ehsan asked.

'When we've eaten,' Ehsan said, 'and it's cooler, we'll walk over to the BLLF offices and I'll introduce you to some of our helpers.'

When the food was brought to him Iqbal ate hungrily, pushing new mouthfuls of rice and bread in before he'd swallowed the previous ones, anxious that it might be taken away from him again.

'You don't have to rush,' Ehsan laughed. 'No one is going to steal your food here, and there'll always be more if you're still hungry.'

'Sorry,' Iqbal said through his mouthful and started to move as if in slow motion to show better manners. But within a minute his speed had increased again and his plate was clean, while Ehsan was still only halfway through his. He refused a second helping, even though he wanted one, feeling self-conscious about appearing greedy, and waited patiently until it was time for them to walk across town to the offices.

The sun was setting and some of the heat was subsiding. The streets teemed with traffic and people coming out for the evening, making Iqbal feel nervous. He half expected the carpet master to suddenly appear and snatch him back. His eyes kept darting from one side to the other, taking in everything. Ehsan walked at a brisk pace, making Iqbal run to keep up as they wove their way down alleys and round corners. Eventually they came to a grand crescent of buildings, which had stood for nearly a century and was now showing its age, battered by sun, rain and neglect. Ehsan led the way to some steps on one corner, which rose up to an entrance. Most of the steps were covered in a stall selling tobacco, sweets and a dazzling variety of other goods. Iqbal had never been inside a building of such splendour and his eyes widened still further at the thought of what might be awaiting him inside.

Salesmen and hawkers swarmed all around the area, some of them selling petrol from a couple of pumps in the middle of the crescent, others selling parking spaces around the edges or just asking for money. Ehsan marched through the entrance and up a staircase to the landing above, which ran all around the first floor of the crescent, providing an elevated pathway to the doors of all the tenants. Men sat on chairs outside the doors, talking to one another or just gazing at the street scene below, waiting for something to happen.

'They're nearly all lawyers and advocates up here,' Ehsan said, but Iqbal had no idea what either word meant, he was too busy trying to catch his breath after the brisk walk. 'If you work hard at school, perhaps you could become like them.'

Iqbal looked back at the men and noticed how new and clean their shirts looked. They were mostly neatly shaved and wore watches too. Some of them even wore socks inside their shoes, despite the heat. He thought he might enjoy being like them.

They turned into another entrance, leading down an alley with yet more office doorways. The last door on the landing proved to be their destination and as Ehsan led the way in, Iqbal was overwhelmed by the number of people crammed into the one tiny room. There were seats round two walls and a desk on another, with every spare inch filled with bodies. Everyone was talking at once, exchanging news, agitated and excited.

Ehsan exchanged a few words with various people without breaking his stride and took Iqbal's hand, leading him through the crowd towards a stone spiral staircase in the corner of the room. The stairs were steep, similar to the ones which went over the kitchen at home in Muridke, and brought them out onto the roof.

The lights of the city around them made the sky glow and Iqbal could hear the noises from the street rising up from below, mainly shouting voices, beeping car horns and roaring engines. There were groups of children sitting on mats around the roof. They all stood up when they saw Ehsan coming out of the stairwell and ran over, the bolder ones chattering with news, the younger ones hanging back and watching. Iqbal could feel their eyes on him, assessing him, working out who he was. He felt suddenly shy and far from home.

'This is Iqbal,' Ehsan told them. 'What do we want him to know?'

With one voice the children on the roof raised their arms, punching the air with their little fists.

'We are free!' they cried. 'We are free!'

Ehsan lifted Iqbal's hand and smiled at him, 'You say it.'

'We are free!' Iqbal said, quietly, and the words felt good in his mouth. He raised both his hands towards the night sky and shouted at the top of his voice. 'We are free!' making the other children laugh and applaud.

CHAPTER SEVEN

GOING BACK FOR THE OTHERS

Iqbal slept so deeply that night when they got back to the Freedom Campus that he was still unconscious when the other children started to filter into the pink hall for school the next morning. He had asked Ehsan the night before if he should sleep with the other rescued children on the roof.

'If you prefer,' Ehsan had smiled, 'but you might be more comfortable inside. They will all be moving on in the next few days, going back to their families.'

'Will I be moving on?' Iqbal asked.

'Only if you want to,' Ehsan had said. 'Or you could stay and help me with my work.'

He opened his eyes to find a circle of curious faces looking down at him, making him jump. He sat up, uncertain where he was or what to say, feeling suddenly uneasy about being in such a new environment, surrounded by unfamiliar faces. The other children seemed equally nonplussed as to what to say to him, so they just stared. From the back of the crowd there was a flurry of activity and four women waded their way through, clucking and tutting at the children, sending them scurrying around the room about their business. The one who reached him first was Mrs Malik, a woman in her middle years with prominent teeth and thick, bushy eyebrows. Iqbal said nothing, waiting to see what would happen next. He knew how hard angry women could hit when they were annoyed by small children, he'd learned that in his own family. He had no wish to be the brunt of any attacks if he could avoid it.

'Young man,' Mrs Malik said, sternly, 'school is about to start. You will be in my group, we assemble over there.'

She pointed him to the far corner of the room and he noticed that the children were dividing up into four groups, more or less according to their size. They were arranging themselves in neat rows, each group facing one of the women. There was very little noise, all of them quiet and attentive, eager to hear what their teachers were going to say to them. Iqbal took a place in the front row of the group Mrs Malik had directed him towards and waited with interest to see what would happen next.

'This is Iqbal,' she told the other children. He was surprised she knew his name. He realised Ehsan must have talked to her about him, a thought that made him glow with pride. He remembered how Ehsan had praised him the night before and wondered if he had said the same to Mrs Malik.

'He's going to be joining our class and we're going to help him to catch up, aren't we?' she said.

The other children gave their half-hearted agreement. It didn't sound as if this was the first time they'd heard such a request. Iqbal looked around at them but they didn't seem to be taking much notice of him, as if they were used to him already. He immediately felt more relaxed and very curious – he had never been to school before. He remembered passing by a school in the village when he was small, peering in through the gates at the bigger children, wondering what they were learning and fully expecting to be there himself one day. Now it seemed he was to be given the chance.

Classes that day lasted for five hours and Iqbal under-stood almost nothing that was said to him. He was sure that if he just concentrated hard enough the lessons that Mrs Malik was giving him would start to make sense; that he would begin to learn. For the time being, however, he could do no more than let the knowledge simply wash over him, hoping it would sweep his ignorance away like dirt beneath a hosepipe. Ehsan had explained to him the previous evening just how important it was that he got an education.

'If you can read and write,' Ehsan said, 'and do some simple sums at least, then no one else can trick you into signing a contract that makes you a slave again. The world is full of moneylenders and slave drivers and unscrupulous people who will always take advantage of the uneducated. Once you have an education you will be able to go back to your village and help your family and neighbours to understand more about their rights in the world, so they can protect themselves against people like your carpet master. Every village needs some educated people in it, to teach the others. That's the only way we can change the way things are.'

Iqbal liked the idea of changing the way things were. During the night, as he lay on the mat in the big pink room, he'd imagined what it would be like to be educated and able to move about the world like Ehsan, confident and able to look everyone in the eye without fear. He remembered his family and neighbours and how they had shouted at the car as he was being driven away. They had been so angry and they seemed so helpless to do anything. All they could do was shout or resort to violence, but it did them no good. They were born, lived and died in the same houses, doing the same jobs or just sitting around waiting for something to happen, never able to escape unless someone else helped them.

Meeting Ehsan was a chance for him to escape that life. Then he could go back and help others. He imagined being able to teach Sobya how to read and write, maybe even bringing her to the city so she could meet and marry an educated man, perhaps one of those lawyers Ehsan had pointed out to him, who would treat her kindly and help her look after their children. Then the children would go to school and would become lawyers as well. The poverty of their mother's childhood would become a distant memory, something they read about in school history books.

It was an exciting and frightening opportunity and he quite expected to have it snatched away from him at any moment. He still became nervous if he heard men's angry raised voices in the distance, imagining the carpet master or a policeman might burst in at any moment and he would be bundled away, watched by all the other children, the teachers ultimately helpless in the face of authority.

Now, as he looked around the room at the other eighty or so little faces staring up at their teachers, he wondered if the same thoughts were going through all their minds. The slate boards they held and wrote upon were the key to their future and they hugged them close to their chests.

At the beginning of the day Iqbal kept quiet and avoided making eye contact with anyone. He was frightened that if they found out he didn't understand half of the things Mrs Malik was saying they'd shout at him and hit him. After a while he realised none of the teachers were carrying sticks, but he was sure that if he displeased them in any way by not working hard enough the sticks would appear and he would be beaten, just as he was so many times at the factory. The strain of concentrating on words that made no sense to him made his head ache, and no matter how hard he tried he still couldn't work out what they were talking about much of the time.

Slowly, however, his confidence grew when he heard nothing but kind words of encouragement coming from the teachers' lips. He saw other children getting things wrong and Mrs Malik merely correcting them. Some of the pupils around him even whispered to one another and giggled behind their hands when they thought she wasn't watching. Iqbal wished they wouldn't do that; it seemed so disrespectful. To have done such a thing at the carpet factory would have resulted in the most terrible repercussions. But the fact that they weren't frightened of Mrs Malik raised his confidence still further.

As he relaxed, he realised the things he was listening to were starting to make more sense. After an hour or two he found the courage to ask questions when he didn't understand what was being said. The questions were met with such politeness and patience that he lost all self-consciousness and settled down to enjoy the experience of learning, his hand going up every few minutes.

At the end of the lessons the children emptied out of the hall, collecting their shoes from the piles outside the door and vanishing back to their other lives, leaving Iqbal standing alone, wondering what to do next.

'Iqbal,' Mrs Malik came out of one of the smaller rooms down the corridor and spotted him, 'would you like to come back to my house for tea and a little television perhaps?'

'Thank you. Yes, I would really like that,' he replied.

'Good, then you can be my escort home.' She sailed out the door, modestly pulling her scarf up over her hair as Iqbal trotted obediently behind her.

Her house was only a few minutes walk from the campus, down an alley of tall buildings, which created a permanent shade for those who lived on the ground floor. The front room of Mrs Malik's house was open to the street and the television was already on, showing cartoons. A girl of about Iqbal's age sat at the table, staring at the flickering screen. Iqbal had glimpsed televisions through other people's doors and windows before, but he had never been invited to actually sit down and watch one. He found it hard to decide whether to stare at the screen, the girl or the surroundings. He wanted to take in everything at once, but it made his head spin.

'Iqbal,' Mrs Malik announced as she squeezed past the table into the tiny room, 'this is my daughter, Fatima. Sit with her while I make some tea.'

Fatima glanced at him for a second before returning her eyes to the television, leaving Iqbal free to look around the room. He liked what he saw. It was a clean, friendly seeming room and it looked as if Mrs Malik and Fatima spent most of their time there. He felt very comfortable. Fatima laughed at something on the screen and he followed her rapt gaze. Within a few seconds the cartoon had captured his attention and he had forgotten all the other distractions as he sat watching, with his mouth hanging open.

'Can you play badminton?' Fatima asked when the cartoon had finished and an adult came onto the screen, sitting in front of a map, talking about something neither of them understood.

'Would you teach me?' he asked.

'Okay. After tea.'

'Were you in school today?' he asked, examining her face more closely, trying to remember if he had seen her in the crowd sitting behind him.

'Yes, but I don't go to the same school as you,' she said. 'Your school is only for dhalits. I go to the proper school.'

Iqbal had heard his family referred to as dhalits before and knew it meant they were at the bottom of the social pile, but somehow if didn't seem offensive when Fatima said it, just matter of fact. He imagined that most of the children working in slavery came from the same class as him. Now he looked at her more closely he could see she was different from all the children who had been in the hall. Her hair was clean and brushed, her clothes new and freshly pressed. He could smell how fresh she was, even from the other side of the table. It was a nice smell.

'Your mother is a very good teacher,' he said.

'I expect she is,' Fatima nodded. 'She's very intelligent. If she wasn't a woman I think she'd be working very high up in the government. But women aren't much better off than slaves in this country, so she does good work instead, educating poor children.'

'I think I'll learn a lot from her,' Iqbal said, liking the way Fatima said exactly what was on her mind.

'You will if you work hard and listen to what she has to say,' she said, primly.

Another cartoon came on and Fatima went back to watching, while Iqbal examined her profile more closely. It was a very pretty profile.

After they'd eaten the food Mrs Malik prepared for them, Fatima took him out into the street with a pair of badminton racquets and a battered shuttlecock.

'You stand at that end,' she pointed to the far end of the alley, 'and try to hit it back to me.'

Proudly showing off her well-practised serve, Fatima sent the shuttlecock soaring high into the air. Iqbal watched in awe as it rose above the web of electrical and telephone wires which looped between the houses on either side of the street, before starting to fall towards him. He saw it coming and he tried to get the racquet under it but only managed to catch it on the wooden edge, making an unimpressive clunking sound and sending it sideways into the gutter.

'Don't worry,' Fatima shouted, 'I was useless to begin with. You need to practise, that's all.'

By the time Mrs Malik called Fatima in to do her home-work before going to bed, Iqbal was hitting almost every shot she sent him, although not always in the direction he expected. Sometimes he even hit them squarely on the strings, which was a satisfying feeling. He felt exhilarated from the exercise and flushed with pride at having mastered a new skill.

'Do you think you can find your own way back to the Freedom Campus?' Mrs Malik asked him, as Fatima got her books out on the table.

'Yes, I think so,' he said, doubtfully.

She gave him some brief instructions and sent him on his way. He set off at a brisk pace, to show willing, but as soon as he was round the corner and out of sight he slowed down. He was in no hurry to get back. There was a whole city to be explored and sights to be stared at before he was ready to curl up on his mat in the corner of the pink room again. As he strolled through the streets, gazing into the brightly lit shops and houses, he realised that for the first time in his life he felt completely happy.

The next day Ehsan took Iqbal to one side after school, leading him into one of the small rooms at the campus where another man, wearing a western suit, was waiting.

'I think we should see what we can do for your friends at the carpet factory,' Ehsan said. 'Don't you?'

Iqbal beamed. His former co-workers had been on his conscience ever since he left them. He was sure they would have been forced to make up for the work that should have been his and he felt guilty that he had enjoyed such a change in fortunes while they were still trapped in the dark.

'This gentleman is a lawyer and has agreed to come with me to talk to your former employer. I will need you to show me where the factory is, but you must promise me you will wait in the car while we go in. Do you promise that?'

'Yes, Ehsan,' he said, 'I promise.'

He didn't intend to do anything that might stop Ehsan from trying to free his friends, even though he would dearly have loved to see the look on the faces of his oppressors when he turned up yet again, this time with a genuine helper.

Ehsan had borrowed the same car that he had been in at the rally where Iqbal had first met him, and the lawyer was driving a battered old minibus. They left Lahore in convoy and once they reached the outskirts of Muridke Iqbal directed Ehsan along the route that he had travelled several thousand times during his captivity. The panic that rose in his chest as they drew closer made him want to scream and he had to hold his breath to stop himself. He could only give Ehsan abrupt instructions: 'Over there. Down there. Behind that building. That gate.'

Ehsan drew up and the minibus parked behind him. The gates to the compound were open and Iqbal could see the overseers sitting with their evening cups of tea.

'Okay,' Ehsan said. 'Wait there. This won't take long.'

Iqbal slid low in his seat, so that only his eyes showed above the dashboard as he watched Ehsan striding through the gates, white shirt tails flying, with the lawyer hurrying to keep up.

The overseers sprang to their feet and Iqbal was pleased to see their heads were bowed. They were obviously intimidated by their visitors. Ehsan was doing the talking, pointing at the lawyer who was holding up sheaves of official-looking paper. After a few minutes Ehsan strode on towards the factory doors, apparently instructing one of the overseers to unbolt them for him. Iqbal noticed the other man slinking out of the gates and running down the street. He guessed he'd gone to fetch the owner and his heart thumped even faster. Should he run in and warn Ehsan that the owner was on his way? Or should he stay where he was, as he'd been told? He forced himself to sit still. Everyone had now disappeared and all he could hear was his own heartbeat and breathing as he waited for what seemed like hours.

Ehsan emerged from the factory with the children at the same moment as the owner ran round the corner, buttoning his shirt as he came. Iqbal slid even lower, still watching. He couldn't believe how meek the owner was being. How was it possible that he had been frightened of this man who was now cringing around Ehsan like a guilty schoolboy brought in front of the headmaster? The lawyer was giving the man papers, which the man seemed to be accepting humbly. Where had all his bravado vanished to?

Ehsan was ushering the children across the road to the waiting vehicles and Iqbal slid down a couple more inches as the back door of the car swung open and he heard Ehsan telling some of the children to get in, sending others to get into the minibus.

Only when Ehsan had climbed into the driving seat and started the car, did Iqbal feel safe to sit up and turn round. The back seat was crammed with familiar faces, all of them looking confused. When they saw him their puzzlement seemed to deepen even further. He could see in their eyes that they looked on him as being different from them. Even though they had spent so many years together in the same predicament, they didn't see him as one of them any more. They saw him as being connected to the grown-up world, the one that made the decisions about their lives, about whether they should work or be free.

'My friend has set you free,' he said, proudly. 'You're going to be able to go back to your families. My friend will arrange for you to go to school.'

He felt a weight lifting from his conscience. They were going to be free, and it was all because of him. His heart soared.

Chapter Eight

Planning a Succession

Apart from Fatima, who he had his tea with most evenings, Iqbal found he had little time to spend with the other children outside of class. There was so much to learn from being around Ehsan and the other adults at the BLLF; so many questions that needed answers. To begin with, the adults were a little self-conscious going about their normal business with Iqbal's piercing eyes on them, sucking in every piece of information they let slip, but after a while they grew used to him being there, asking questions, pestering them to give him tasks to perform, no matter how humble.

He loved being given jobs because they provided him with excuses to find out more about Lahore, about the organisation and about the people he'd suddenly found himself living amongst. As he ran around the streets on errands, delivering messages, picking up shopping, fetching cups of tea, he couldn't understand why so many men seemed content to just sit around all day, smoking and staring into space. Didn't they have things they wanted to achieve? People they wanted to help? Questions they wanted answers to?

Children's games puzzled him almost as much; not the structured skills of games like badminton, but the apparently aimless hours other children spent on make-believe and just running around, laughing and chasing one another. Iqbal tried to join in during the break times between lessons, but he couldn't see the point of such activity when there were so many more interesting things to be doing and finding out. By the end of every break he was nearly always back beside an adult, wearing them out with his earnest discussions.

'Iqbal,' Mrs Malik teased him one day, 'do you never think you should give that poor brain of yours a rest? You'll wear it out with all this thinking.'

'Will I?' he asked, his shocked expression making her laugh.

'No,' she assured him, 'not really, but sometimes it is good for a brain to rest. Why don't you run around with the others for a while?'

He had agreed, reluctantly, to do as she suggested, but after a few minutes he had become bored again and mooched off to one of the smaller rooms to see if Ehsan or one of the other men were there.

Whenever Ehsan was in Lahore, Iqbal would stick as close to him as he possibly could. Without putting it in so many words, even to himself, he could think of no better man to become than Ehsan Khan. He wanted to understand every thought that went through his saviour's head.

The more time the boy spent around him, the more Ehsan found himself talking to him as if he was an equal, forgetting that he was still only ten years old.

'How did you become interested in freeing slaves?' Iqbal asked one afternoon when the two of them were standing on the roof of the BLLF office, watching the kites dipping and diving over the city.

'I was a seventeen-year-old student and I knew nothing about the way people were enslaved in Pakistan,' Ehsan said, his eyes fixed on the dancing kites as his memory slid back over the years. He'd told the story hundreds of times, but it still seemed as fresh as if it had happened yesterday. 'I'd learned about the slaves in America and had thought that when they were freed that was the end of slavery. Most people live with it going on all around them and just don't see it. I was the same, too busy with my own life to ask the right questions and really think things through. I had seen children at work and never given it a second thought; it seemed so normal. I was training to be a journalist and I knew there were many bad things happening that I wanted to expose, but I was not focused. I hadn't had my eyes opened.'

'So who opened them for you?' Iqbal asked after a few moments' silence.

'There was an old man trying to get across the road and I stopped to help him,' Ehsan said. 'He moved slowly because his body was so worn out, and we got talking during our long journey through the traffic. His heart was full of sadness, which he wanted to share, and by the time we reached the other side of the road he'd made me want to hear more. We went to a tea stall and I bought him a drink and listened as he told me his story.'

'Was he a slave?' Iqbal asked, impatient with his friend for taking so long to get to the point of his story.

'He'd been a worker at one of the brick kilns all his life. All his family, including his two daughters, worked there too. Their owner was cruel and didn't pay them, keeping them prisoner. Now I know it is all too common a story, but then I was shocked, not even sure if I could believe him. When he discovered that his daughters were being raped by the owner, the old man had finally decided to rebel and the whole family escaped.'

Iqbal nodded his understanding. He knew all about the chains, both mental and real, that stopped uneducated workers escaping from tyrannical bosses. He was pretty sure he understood about rape too, having watched some of the girls in the factory being taken out by the overseers, and seen them coming back in, crying and ashamed, unable to walk steadily.

'And they came to the city?' he prompted Ehsan.

'He'd reached the city, but his daughters had been recaptured and taken back. They were still being held prisoner by the owner, and raped regularly. The old man had been to the police but he didn't have any money to give them so they beat him up and threw him back out onto the street.'

Iqbal could certainly believe that after his own brief experience at the police station. He felt angry on behalf of this man he'd never met.

'I think he was telling his story to everyone who would listen,' Ehsan continued, 'in the hope that someone would offer to help.'

'And so you offered?'

'I didn't think I could walk away from him. Just helping him across the road and buying him a cup of tea wasn't going to be enough. I went back to my university and I rounded up as many of my friends as I could. Not everyone wanted to help because they were afraid they would jeopardise their careers and enrage their families if they got into trouble, but I found enough. Students are the best people to protest about anything because they're educated but have less to lose than family men and women. You don't want to upset the police if you have a wife and children who could be rounded up and put into prison, or if you have a family dependent on you to provide a living.

'Anyway, we went to the police station in the area of the brick kiln with placards and we surrounded it, shouting slogans, singing songs, demanding they did something about rescuing these two girls.'

'Weren't you frightened they'd put you in prison?' Iqbal found it hard to imagine finding the courage to actually annoy the police when they had so many guns and so little patience.

'I was very young. I still believed you could make people do the right thing if you showed them the way,' Ehsan said, a little sadly.

'Do you not still believe it?'

Ehsan didn't answer, just stared at the kites.

'What happened to the girls?' Iqbal prompted again.

'They were rescued. The police didn't want any fuss and it wasn't a hard job for them. The owner didn't put up a struggle when half a dozen armed policemen turned up at his house, he just handed them over.'

'So it was a great victory,' Iqbal said, rubbing his hands with satisfaction.

'It was a tiny victory, but it made me realise just how widespread the problem was. I realised there were hundreds of thousands of people, including children, who were in the same position, and so I began campaigning, getting as many people as possible to join in. Initially I thought we could solve everything by forcing a change in the law, but once we'd succeeded in doing that I realised it wasn't going to make much difference. No one cared enough to enforce the new law, least of all the police. I decided that the only way forward was to free as many children as possible and give them enough education so that they could help others in their families and communities to avoid the same fate. I know now we will not end the problem in my lifetime, maybe not even in yours, but we can start the process. Each child we rescue is another step forward.'

They both fell silent for a while, lost in their own thoughts.

'I want to help,' Iqbal said eventually.

'You will help,' Ehsan assured him, 'by getting an education and spreading the word, and continuing the fight when I'm too old and tired.'

It was the first time Ehsan had actually put into words his thoughts that Iqbal might be his successor in the struggle against slavery.

'No,' Iqbal interrupted, suddenly excited by his own ideas. 'I want to help now. I want to help you go into the factories and get the children out. If someone like me had come to the carpet factory and told us about our rights we would have listened and been ready to leave when the adults from BLLF arrived. I'm small, it'll be easier for me to get into these places without being seen and to talk to the children without frightening them.'

'No,' Ehsan laughed, 'you concentrate on your education. These raids are very dangerous, the factory owners often have guns and many don't hesitate to use them if they think they're going to lose their best workers. They aren't all as weak as your carpet master, caving in at the first sight of a lawyer. Some of them fight like madmen. The last thing we want is for you to get shot before your life has even started.'

Iqbal stared up at the kites, his lips becoming a thin line of determination. He had too much respect for Ehsan to argue with him any more. He was just going to have to prove to him that he was wrong.

CHAPTER NINE

RESCUE MISSION

Because Iqbal was around the BLLF office so much, Ehsan sometimes forgot he was there. There were so many people coming and going all through the day and night, distracting him with their problems, and Iqbal just seemed like part of the furniture. A lot of the time, of course, he was reminded by the constant stream of questions that poured from the small boy's mouth, as his thirst for knowledge grew and multiplied with every new thing he learned. During the times when Iqbal fell silent and thoughtful, however, Ehsan would go back to talking openly to whoever came to the office to see him, as if Iqbal's dark, serious eyes weren't constantly watching and his large ears weren't listening to every word.

So it was that Iqbal learned of the planned raid on a brick kiln about a hundred miles from Lahore. News of this particular kiln's existence had come from a woman who had escaped and walked all the way to the city, a journey that had taken her nearly two weeks. Iqbal had been in the office when she arrived, shuffling through the office door one afternoon. She'd worn her shoes away on the journey and Iqbal noticed her feet were hard like rocks, with no flesh left on them. There was no flesh on her anywhere that he could see, just burned black skin clinging to the bones of her face and wrists, the only parts of her body that weren't swathed in filthy rags. Later Ehsan told him that she was only about forty years old, but she looked more like a hundred to Iqbal.

Her name was Maya and she'd been brought into the office by Mrs Baber, who'd found her passed out against the wall on the walkway outside. Having revived her with a little rice and water, she gradually coaxed her story out of her. She then brought her to meet Ehsan and insisted she tell the story all over again.

'Tell Mr Khan about your son, Maya,' she prompted, as the woman crouched humbly and silently in the corner of the office, grateful for the chance to sit in some comfortable shade with a cup of tea in her hand, not thinking of asking for any more.

'He's dead,' she said, with no visible emotion.

'Tell him why he is dead,' Mrs Baber insisted. 'If you tell Mr Khan what has happened he can help your other children.'

'The master of the brick kiln killed him,' Maya said, her expression still deadpan.

Iqbal examined her face closely to see if he could see any signs of a tear, but there were none. He could understand that. He knew how it felt to be so tired and so defeated you could no longer find the energy to care about anything, that you no longer had enough energy to expect anything of life.

'How did this happen?' Ehsan asked, his eyes as sad as always, his voice gentler than Mrs Baber's and more encouraging.

'My son found the master with his sister …' The woman sipped her tea and cast her eyes to the floor, ashamed to say any more.

'How old is your daughter, Maya?' Ehsan asked.

The woman shrugged. 'About ten years old,' she said. 'She's my youngest. She's not old. The master used her as a servant in his house, as well as making her work in the kiln. But he raped her and my son saw it. My son tried to stop him because his sister was crying. The master was very angry and beat my son to death with an iron bar. Now he doesn't allow any of us to talk to my daughter or see her any more.'

Iqbal imagined how he would feel if he had found Sobya in such a position. He could understand exactly why the brother would have taken the risk of standing up to protect her, even if he was bound to be beaten for his insolence. It would be impossible to know such a thing was going on and not do anything to stop it.

'What about your husband?' Ehsan asked.

'He died. The dust was in his lungs and he wasn't able

to breathe any more,' she said, matter-of-factly. 'The dust kills everyone in the end. Only the children are left.'

'How many work at this man's kiln?'

The woman looked towards Mrs Baber for help with the numbers.

'I think there must be about twelve children there,' Mrs Baber said, 'not just in the kiln but working for him in other capacities. She has two other sons there.'

'Would you be able to take us back to the kiln?' Ehsan asked the woman. 'Would you be able to remember the route?'

'Every step of it,' she said, with the smallest flash of a smile, as if she sensed she had finally found someone who was willing to help her, but hardly dared to believe it could be true.

'You won't have to walk this time,' Mrs Baber explained, patting her hand comfortingly.

Iqbal didn't bother to ask Ehsan if he could go with him on the mission, because he knew the answer would be no. He just made sure that from then on he was always around when they were discussing it. He became adept at pretending to be absorbed in some task, while at the same time listening to every phone call and conversation, adjusting his own plans as he went along.

A man he'd never heard of before was recruited because he had a truck big enough to hold twelve children as well as the adults who were going to be travelling to free

them. Iqbal made a mental note of the man's name so he
would know when he was being talked about. A time and
a date were set for their departure, but Iqbal still managed
to give no indication he was paying attention. They were
going to leave late in the evening, once the heat had gone
out of the sun, in the hope the owner would be asleep by
the time they reached their destination. It would be hard
waking everyone else without waking him, but it was still
the best way of taking him by surprise. Iqbal took in all of
this, but still he said nothing.

All through that day he was quieter than normal at
school, as if lost in thought. Mrs Malik, used to him being
the liveliest pupil in her group, asked him if he was feeling
quite well.

'Yes, thank you,' he replied, with a smile that seemed a
little forced to her. She wondered what was troubling the
boy and decided to question Fatima about it later. Having
checked that he felt all right, Mrs Malik left him to his
thoughts. In some ways it was a bit of a relief when Iqbal
stopped asking questions for a while. She was becoming
increasingly aware that there would soon be a time when
he would be asking things she did not have answers for.
It would be a sad day for her when she had to admit she
had nothing else to teach him and had to hand him on
to someone new; she had never encountered a child with
such a propensity for learning before. She could understand why Ehsan had singled him out from the others

and was paying him so much attention. The boy had a potential she had never seen in the hundreds of dull-eyed, broken-spirited children she had seen passing through the BLLF schoolrooms. A return to freedom and school revived some of their childish spark, but none of them had the intense determination of this child.

She used the day to concentrate on some of the other children whose needs were in danger of being overshadowed by the voracious curiosity of their classmate.

At the end of the classes he went back with her for tea with Fatima, still strangely uncommunicative. He declined their usual game of badminton, claiming he was tired and wanted to return to the Freedom Campus to sleep.

'Are you sure you're all right?' Mrs Malik asked again. 'You don't seem your usual self.'

'I think perhaps I'm just tired,' Iqbal replied, giving a theatrical yawn as if to prove his point. 'I'll be better by tomorrow.'

Mrs Malik looked sceptical but said no more as Fatima didn't appear to have noticed anything unusual about her young friend's behaviour.

However, instead of returning to Freedom Campus, when Iqbal left them he walked to the parking area outside the BLLF office, standing in the shadows of the arch that led through to the park, watching to see what would happen. He knew he was early, but he wanted to be sure of exactly what was going on. His heart was thumping in his chest almost as hard as it had on the night he'd escaped from the factory, which now seemed a lifetime ago, even though it was just a matter of months. He felt bad that he was deceiving Ehsan, but he was determined to prove he would be an asset on missions like these.

There were so many vans and small lorries coming and going he couldn't work out which one was going to be the one for the mission. After an hour of watching, his patience was rewarded when Ehsan and a young lawyer came out of the main door and down the steps. A man who had previously been squatting on the bottom stair sprang to his feet and shook them both by the hand. Maya, the woman from the kiln, followed behind them looking small and frightened, shrouded in scarves as if trying to make herself invisible.

The three men made their way towards an open truck that Iqbal had seen the man from the steps draw up in a few minutes earlier. Iqbal felt a surge of relief, mixed with a rush of excitement. If they'd been travelling in a covered minibus of some sort it would have been impossible for him to stow away; now there was a chance he would be able to get on board without being spotted.

This would be the hardest part of the operation. If they caught him at this stage they would refuse to take him and they would be cross with him for being disobedient. It would be much easier to persuade Ehsan to let him take part in the rescue operation once they were actually there.

But could he get into the truck undetected? If the three men were going to be in the cab he didn't think they would be able to see what was going on behind them. There was a chance he might be able to smuggle himself aboard without being seen in the few seconds between them getting in and drawing away. Every muscle in his body was tight with anticipation.

All four adults squeezed into the cab, Maya pulling her scarf low across her eyes to cover her embarrassment at being pressed so close to the men. Iqbal moved out of the shadows and darted between the parked cars until he was just behind the truck, bending low to keep out of the line of the rear-view mirrors. He waited for the driver to reverse out of his parking space, afraid he would be spotted if the man was looking backwards. It took a few manoeuvres before the driver had managed to get past other haphazardly parked vehicles and into a position where he could draw away. Finally he was pointing in the right direction.

As the truck accelerated forward towards the traffic of the main road, Iqbal sprinted out behind it. He was expecting it to stop before entering the stream of other cars, which would give him time to clamber over the tailgate while the people in the cab were all concentrating on the busy road ahead.

The driver, however, was not one for the niceties of traffic laws. He pushed his way in without touching the brakes, forcing other cars and bikes already in the stream to swerve around him. Iqbal's chest ached with the strain of running so fast but still he managed to find a tiny bit more speed. He grabbed hold of a handle on the tailgate. The truck accelerated again, dragging him off his feet for a second. The hard surface of the road grazed the skin of his legs painfully before he was able to right himself. Unable now to let go, for fear of falling under the wheels of the cars behind, Iqbal pulled himself up so his feet were on the bumper and launched himself over the side. He landed heavily on the floor of the truck amongst a selection of old car engine parts.

He lay still for several minutes, partly to wait and see if the men in the cab had heard or seen anything, and partly because he had no breath left in him. As the dizziness passed, the pain from his legs became more intense, but he managed to sit up, leaning against the side of the truck, and braced himself as it swerved and bumped its way out of Lahore into the darkness of the countryside.

The journey seemed to take forever. By the time they finally stopped at the side of a road, he was covered with bruises from the many sharp corners on the machinery lying around him. Iqbal sat up and looked around him but could see no lights at all. When the driver turned off his headlights the darkness was total. The doors of the cab opened and the adults climbed out. Iqbal pulled himself to his feet, unsure how best to let Ehsan know he was there. A torch clicked on and the beam swung around the ground beside the truck. He could hear whispering but couldn't make out what they were saying.

'Ehsan,' he hissed and the beam of light swung up into his eyes, blinding him.

'What are you doing here?' Ehsan whispered back.

'I came to help.'

'I told you this work is too dangerous. You could get hurt.'

Iqbal was surprised he didn't sound more angry. 'I'm already hurt from riding in the truck. Where's the kiln?'

There was a moment's silence as Ehsan considered the situation before he seemed to decide he had no option other than to include the boy in the mission. 'Maya says it's just behind these trees,' he replied.

'I'll go in first and find the children,' Iqbal said, climbing out of the truck and dropping to the ground, biting his lip to stop himself from exclaiming at the spasm of pain the movement sent through his body. It seemed natural that he should have a plan and the adults didn't argue with him.

'Be very careful, Iqbal,' Ehsan said. 'This man has killed at least one boy already.'

'But you'll be here to save me,' Iqbal replied, matter-of-factly.

They said nothing further as they made their way through the trees, leaving the driver guarding the truck. Maya was letting out little whimpering noises as they got closer and a sliver of light appeared in front of them.

'That's the owner's home,' she said. 'My daughter sleeps under the house. The others are in that building there.'

They all strained their eyes to make out the building she was pointing towards.

'Are you sure you want to do this?' Ehsan asked Iqbal.

'Of course,' Iqbal replied. He couldn't think of anything he wanted to do more.

'We'll wait ten minutes, but if you get into trouble just shout and we'll come immediately.'

Iqbal didn't hesitate and two minutes later he was beside the building where the workers were sleeping, all his pains forgotten in the excitement. His eyes were accustoming themselves to the dark. There was enough light from the moon, which had appeared from behind some cloud, to make out where the door was, but not enough to see how it was fastened. It took several minutes of fumbling, scraping his knuckles painfully in the process, before he managed to locate and draw back the bolts, which had been designed to keep the workers there until it was time to start work in the morning.

The noises of metal against metal were enough to disturb the sleep of those inside and several anxious pairs of eyes blinked out of the blackness as he pulled open the door. Iqbal knew exactly what they were thinking. He remembered how it felt whenever someone opened the factory door; how they all tensed, expecting a beating or an angry tirade. Sometimes the owner would come in and he would have a smile spread across his face, but that would usually mean he'd just received a big new order and had come to share the good news with them. He would then tell them it would mean they had to work through the night, or through their meal break. All news was bad news when you worked in one of these places.

'Don't be frightened,' he whispered. 'My name's Iqbal Masih. I've come to set you free. The owner of this kiln is breaking the law by forcing you to stay here. I represent an organisation called the Bonded Labour Liberation Front. We can help you to escape and lead a free life.'

None of them made any response, either fearing he was tricking them or else simply not being able to comprehend what he was saying. He realised it would be hard for them to take in his words when they had just woken up.

'I used to work like you,' he tried again, 'in a carpet factory, and the BLLF rescued me and put me into a school so I could get an education. If you come with me you can learn to read and write as well. I'm not on my own here, there's a truck and a lawyer and Maya, who brought us here to get you all out.'

The mention of Maya's name caused a stirring in the darkness and Iqbal was able to make out the shapes of several children coming forward.

'Maya's come back for us?' one of them asked in a small voice.

'Maya has brought us here to rescue you,' he said.

Still they seemed uncertain, nervous at the prospect of stepping outside their known surroundings without the permission of the owner, the man who made all the decisions in their lives.

'If you want to leave,' Iqbal said, 'get yourselves ready and the men will be down to help us in a minute. I have to find Maya's daughter.'

'She sleeps under the house,' a child's whisper told him, 'with the others.'

'The others?'

'He keeps all the girls over there.'

'Are they locked in?' Iqbal asked.

'Where would they go?' the voice replied. 'They're girls.'

His eyes finally well adjusted to the gloom, Iqbal left the hut, which was now buzzing with uncertain whisperings and mutterings, and made his way across to the house that Maya had pointed out. None of the moon's weak light penetrated the pitch-blackness beneath the building. The gap couldn't have been more than two feet between the ground and the floorboards above. Iqbal lay on his stomach and edged his way into the unknown. It smelled bad, like a rat had died.

'Hello?' he hissed, aware the owner and his family might be sleeping only inches away above his head. 'Are you there?'

He wished he'd taken the time to find out what Maya's daughter's name was.

'Maya's daughter, are you there?'

He could hear a noise. He paused, trying to work out which direction it had come from. It sounded like someone was trying to stifle their sobbing.

'Don't be afraid,' he said. 'Maya's sent me to fetch you and take you to somewhere safe.'

He could remember the looks on the faces of the girls in the carpet factory when they came out from being in the back room with the overseers, the blank expressions in their eyes and the way they just went back to work without saying a word or looking around. Sometimes he'd been able to see where the tears had left tracks in the dust on their faces. He guessed these girls were in the same state.

The crying sound became louder, cutting through the silence of the night outside and someone stirred above his head. Iqbal couldn't think of any way to quieten whoever was crying without making more noise.

'Shh,' he tried, 'Maya's waiting.'

But the crying had now become a wailing and he could hear footsteps above and the sounds of an angry male voice. He scrambled backwards into the fresher night air.

'Ehsan!' he shouted out into the darkness as a door opened behind him and light oozed out onto the red coloured earth around him. He thought he heard a responding voice from the darkness but couldn't be sure because a blow fell on the back of his neck at the same moment, sending him sprawling forward in the dirt. A bare foot landed as hard as a boot in his ribs, and then another one.

'Piss off, you little troublemaker,' a voice said before kicking him again.

Trying to roll away out of reach, Iqbal looked up and saw that the figure attacking him was carrying a gun. It must have been the butt of the gun that had knocked him to the floor. The wailing from under the house had stopped with a terrible suddenness and Iqbal could imagine whoever was under there was now straining their ears, trying to work out what was happening outside.

The foot hit his ribs again, just as another voice caused his assailant to turn and point his gun at the unseen intruder on his property.

'My name is Ehsan Khan from the Bonded Labour Liberation Front,' the voice announced and Iqbal scrambled out of the pool of light on all fours, the pain from his ribs stabbing like knives. 'We've come to inform your workers that they're free to leave at any time they like, that they have no debt to you because the government has cancelled it and made such an arrangement illegal.'

While the owner was busy trying to work out where Ehsan's voice was coming from, swinging the barrel of the gun back and forth, Iqbal scurried back to the hut. He could see that several of the inmates had come to the door, which he'd left open, and were peering out, trying to see what was happening.

'If you want to leave,' he said, 'come out now.'

Ehsan and the lawyer had stepped out of the darkness into the pool of light outside the house and Maya had run past them, falling on her hands and knees and screaming to her daughter under the house. It was possible to see the owner's face now, contorted with anger as he turned one way and another, trying to work out where to exert his authority first.

'Stay inside,' he roared at his workers, but some of them had plucked up their courage and were emerging from the door, watching Maya. The owner swung round and pointed his gun at the prone woman.

'Get away from the house!' he roared, but she didn't stop her frantic pleadings and Iqbal could see the faces of three small girls emerging from the gap. As the first one came out Maya grabbed her and hugged her tightly. The owner obviously changed his mind about where to direct his wrath and swung round to face Ehsan and the lawyer again, releasing a shot from his rifle into the air above the intruders' heads. Everyone ducked back for a moment and the man took the opportunity to shout instructions all around him, ordering Ehsan off his property and everyone else back to their sleeping places.

Ehsan straightened himself up again and repeated his opening words. Iqbal urged the workers from the hut to move forward a few more feet and Maya ran across to Ehsan, with her daughter running beside her as if sheltering from the rain beneath her mother's ragged skirts. The two other little girls ran behind.

'Get back!' the owner screamed, his voice becoming shrill with anger as he raised his rifle to his shoulder and took aim at them.

'Don't fire or you'll be in prison for murder,' Ehsan shouted.

'Quickly!' Iqbal hissed at the workers.

Their courage seemed to arrive in a flood as they all followed Maya's lead and headed towards Ehsan.

'Take them to the truck,' Ehsan told Iqbal as soon as he saw they had a chance of getting away. 'We'll follow.'

Now he was close, Iqbal could see the lawyer was shaking so much with fear that the papers he was holding in his hand were rattling, but Ehsan appeared to be fearless, as if it didn't occur to him for a second that the man would ever dare to shoot him.

The owner was left raging on his empty property as Iqbal and Maya led the way back through the trees to the road. They heard some more shots being fired but had no way of knowing if they had found a target. The important thing was to get everyone onto the truck as quickly as possible. If Ehsan or the lawyer had been wounded or killed then they would have to fetch help anyway.

The sounds of shots were more than the driver's nerves could stand. Waiting alone in the darkness had been hard enough. Iqbal heard an engine revving and saw the tail lights of the truck come on. It started to move away and he increased his pace, despite the pain in his legs and his ribs, shouting at the man to stop, trying to make his voice heard above the roar of the engine.

Just when he thought his lungs were going to explode, Iqbal saw the brake lights come on and the truck jolted to a stop. He didn't take the time to explain anything to the driver, just helped the escaping workers to climb over the tailboard. No one was speaking, all of them surrendering themselves into the hands of strangers with no idea where they would be taken next or what would happen to them. Iqbal could imagine how frightened they were. He could remember what a leap of faith it had been when he first put his trust in Ehsan.

The driver was leaning out of his window shouting that he wanted to go. He hadn't expected to be involved in a gunfight in the middle of nowhere. He hadn't expected to find himself in this sort of danger; Ehsan had just asked him to help out carrying some children. He had a wife and family at home who depended on him for their existence, he couldn't afford to take a bullet and be unable to work.

'Wait for Ehsan Khan,' Iqbal pleaded, 'he's coming behind us.'

'He's been shot,' the driver said, 'we need to get out before we're all killed!'

Iqbal didn't know what to do. How long should they wait? What if the man was right and it was the owner who appeared through the trees with his gun and not Ehsan? What would happen then? Should he get the children to safety and come back for Ehsan and the lawyer later?

Before he had to make a decision he heard more shouting and running figures came out of the darkness. The driver ducked back into his cab, slamming the truck into gear. Some of the children were crying with fear as Ehsan and the lawyer leapt into the cab, which was jolting towards the highway.

Once they were on the main road and heading back to the city, Iqbal felt a rush of relief and elation at having survived. He decided the children all needed their spirits raising. Lifting his hands in the air, despite the swaying of the truck, he shouted, 'We are free! We are free!' at the top of his voice, urging the children to join him. To begin with it didn't seem that any of them could find the courage to speak so wildly, but Iqbal refused to give up, moving from one to another as best he could, lifting their arms up and smiling broadly as he chanted, over and over again. Within a few miles they were all shouting like they never had before. Voices that had always been suppressed were joyfully expressing themselves for the first time.

CHAPTER TEN

THE LITTLE HERO

Once they reached the glow of the city, Iqbal examined the faces of his fellow travellers more carefully. There were about fifteen of them and they all looked like they could be part of the same family. It was hard to guess their ages since their skins had been stained with brick dust and dried by the constant heat of the kiln – like fruit that has had the life juices sucked from it.

From their size he guessed most of the children were about the same age as him or younger, but there were a few young adults, who looked as worn out and half starved as Maya had when she first turned up at their office. When Maya said there were only children left, maybe they still seemed like children to her, or maybe they were all years younger than they looked.

None of them made eye contact with him, even after joining in the chanting; they all went back to staring straight ahead as soon as he gave up cajoling them into joining in. They showed virtually no curiosity about the street nightlife they were passing by, apparently drained of life. It was as if they'd given up thinking or feeling anything, quite willing to wait for the next thing to happen to them. Perhaps, Iqbal thought, they weren't afraid of the unknown because they believed nothing worse could be done to them than had already been done.

He remembered the other children in the carpet factory behaving the same way, as if their personalities had been beaten out of them. They showed no interest in the outside world because they didn't believe it had anything to do with them. He felt exhilarated by his adventures; the blood was pumping through his veins and he wanted to be able to talk about it with someone, to relive the whole experience with someone again. But no one in the truck wanted to relive anything. He was forced to bottle up his excitement and endure the uncomfortable journey in silence.

By the time they reached the BLLF office it was deep in the night, but the air was still hot once the truck stopped moving and they lost the breeze. Iqbal climbed down first, aware of just how many new bumps and bruises he'd collected since they set out, not just from the beating but from the ride as well. He helped the others down and they all stood together in the road while Ehsan and the lawyer went up to the office to make sure it was open. Iqbal stayed with them like a sheepdog guarding a flock, making sure none of them strayed off and became lost in the city, or were picked off by the predators and denizens of the night he could see hovering in the shadows, watching and waiting their opportunity.

After what seemed like an age, Ehsan returned and told them all to follow him. Mrs Baber was waiting in the office, looking as if she'd been dragged from her bed, which she probably had, and she shooed the docile crowd through the office and up the spiral staircase onto the roof, where mats had been laid out for everyone to sleep. Iqbal guided each of them to a mat and told them that was where they were to rest until the morning. He showed them where the toilet was in the corner of the roof, its privacy guarded by a shabby curtain strung between two makeshift walls. None of them demonstrated any interest in their surroundings or asked any questions. They were like sleep walkers.

Although no one asked it of him, Iqbal sat up all night at the top of the stairs, so that no one could get onto the roof without waking him first. Ehsan assured him it wasn't necessary as the office below would be locked and there was no other way onto the roof, but nodded his agreement when he saw how determined the boy was to stay there. Iqbal felt a personal responsibility for the people on the roof, knowing from his own experience how confused and frightened they must be feeling. He didn't know what he would do if anyone did try to come up the stairs, but he thought his presence there on guard duty might make the others feel safer.

No one came and it was the rising sun that first stirred his sleeping charges. They were already moving around and talking quietly amongst themselves when Mrs Baber arrived up the stairs, struggling for breath and carrying large bowls of food. For the next hour or two she and Iqbal laboured up and down, running messages and fetching food and drink. Iqbal marvelled at her ability to stay so fat when she worked and sweated so hard. The biggest problem for him was the pain in his ribs, but he found that if he kept busy he didn't think about it so much. He liked feeling helpful.

Iqbal was the only one in the office when the men arrived. Because it had been so dark the night before he didn't immediately recognise the owner from the brick kiln, but the moment the man opened his mouth he remembered the voice. If anything the man's anger had grown in the intervening hours, no doubt exacerbated by the long drive into the city and the struggle of finding out where the BLLF office was in the maze of streets. Iqbal guessed he must have been searching since first light. He had with him two ugly looking youths who reminded Iqbal of the overseers he'd known at the carpet factory and he felt a ripple of fear run through him at the memory. These men didn't seem to be willing to accept defeat as easily as his former master had done. He remembered Ehsan's warning about how much of a fight some of these employers would be willing to put up in order to hold on to children they saw as their rightful property.

Somehow, in the light of day, without his gun and away from his own little kingdom, the owner didn't appear as all-powerful, but that made him seem even more dangerous, like a cornered rat. He had a look of desperation in his eyes. The pains in Iqbal's chest and neck reminded him that this was a man who wouldn't hesitate to hurt him.

'Where are they?' the man snarled.

Iqbal opened his mouth but couldn't think of a suitable response.

'Your boss,' the man jabbed him in the chest with a finger, sending the pain shooting through his battered ribs, 'has stolen my workforce. If they're not back at work by the end of the day I'm going to the police.'

'They're people,' Iqbal's anger overcame his fear and found some words for him, 'not your property. They can't be stolen from you. You didn't even pay them for the work they did for you.'

The flat of the man's hand came down across the side of Iqbal's face, sending him hurtling across the room, knocking over the chairs.

'Don't tell me how to run my business. I think the police would be very interested to hear how your boss is sabotaging successful Pakistani businesses. Is he working for the Jews or the Indians? Who is he working for?'

'He's working for the poor people of Pakistan,' Iqbal shouted, unable to stop the tears from choking his voice as he struggled back onto his feet. 'He's working to make Pakistan a great modern country and to abolish slavery.'

'I want to know where my workers are.' The man did not intend to waste his time discussing politics with the sort of boy he held in the lowest of contempt. 'And you are going to tell me.'

Before Iqbal was steady on his feet the two young thugs had followed the nod of their master and were advancing towards him with their fists clenched and a gleam in their eyes, which suggested they were hungry for violence.

'Leave the boy alone.'

Mrs Baber had appeared at the bottom of the staircase, having come down to find out why Iqbal was taking so long to return with the water she needed. In her hand was the knife she'd been cutting up food with for the refugees on the roof. It was a knife she'd been using in her kitchen all her adult life, and her mother had used it before her. It had cut the throats of many animals down the years and it rested in her hand as easily and naturally as an extra thumb. She didn't have to make any threatening gestures to draw the eyes of the men towards the blade that had been sharpened so often and so thoroughly for so long it had become almost transparent.

Both the young thugs moved back behind their boss. Mrs Baber's voice reminded them of the voices of their mothers and grandmothers, women who were used to being obeyed by their children. Iqbal pulled himself upright and dusted himself down, regaining as much dignity as possible as the three intruders lost all of theirs, backing towards the door uttering foolish threats about what they would be doing to both of them when they next met.

The moment they were outside the office door Mrs Baber slammed it angrily and locked it, leaving them outside on the landing, looking confused and frustrated as to what to do next.

'They won't stay for long,' she told Iqbal, and he noticed she was panting from the exertion. 'Ehsan will soon be here and we can move these people to the Freedom Campus until he works out what to do with them.'

'Thank you for helping me,' Iqbal said, his polite words not fully expressing the gratitude he felt towards anyone who was willing to stand up for him in a way his own family had never been prepared to do. Mrs Baber nodded, before taking a deep breath and heading back up the stairs to the roof once more.

By the time Ehsan arrived, the walkway outside the office was empty. Puzzled as to why the door should be locked in the middle of the day, he eventually managed to make himself heard and was let in. Emerging onto the roof he found that Iqbal had constructed what looked like a temporary village, converting the sleeping mats into makeshift shelters from the sun, and was leading the children once more in the 'we are free' chant, as they waved their arms gleefully in the air.

The moment they saw Ehsan their shyness returned and their chanting subsided into a self-conscious mumbling, their hands falling down to their sides and their eyes fixing on the floor. They might have grown sufficiently confident of Iqbal and Mrs Baber to relax their guard, but Ehsan was a man and none of them had any reason to trust men.

Mrs Baber explained to Ehsan what had happened that morning and he nodded thoughtfully as he listened. He didn't seem surprised or alarmed at the thought of the brick kiln master being in the city and looking for trouble. Iqbal wondered if anything ever frightened Ehsan.

When Iqbal came up to him, he put his arm around the boy's shoulders.

'You must be hungry,' he said. 'Let's go for lunch.'

Ehsan led the way down the steps and through the office with Iqbal trotting behind, his eyes flickering into every dark corner in case the brick kiln boss was lying in wait for them. As they emerged from the side alley onto the main walkway above the street Iqbal noticed that people lounging against the balustrade, looking down at the street, were nudging one another and looking in his direction. The lawyers sitting on their chairs in the shade smiled and nodded to him as he passed them in a way they never had before.

On the steps in front of the building one or two children ran up and stood just a few feet from him, staring unashamedly. Iqbal smiled at them and their faces lit up, as if a passing spirit had blessed them. Ehsan, looking forward to his lunch and unaware of what was happening just behind him, strolled the length of the building to the restaurant, which stood at the centre of the crescent, beside the archway leading to the park.

The staff inside saw him approaching and rushed to open the door and usher him in. As Iqbal followed, the children who'd been trailing him stopped at the bottom of the steps, knowing they could go no further as they met the withering looks of the doorman and managers.

Several of the children on the BLLF office roof had also spotted Iqbal and Ehsan leaving. Seeing that Mrs Baber was behind the curtain, busy washing plates in a bowl beside the toilet, the braver ones ventured down the stairs after their new-found friends, the others following in dribs and drabs as their courage built and the roof around them began to look empty. None of them wanted to be left on their own. By the time Mrs Baber realised what was happening the last few were disappearing into the stair door. She shook her head despairingly. Where on earth, she wondered, did they all think they were going to go in a strange city?

The waiters fussed over Iqbal and Ehsan in the restaurant, taking their orders and recommending the best dishes of the day. They knew Ehsan well and if he chose to bring an urchin through the doors for lunch he must have a reason. There had been stories of how he'd once taken a group of freed slave children into the Pearl Continental Hotel for tea, ignoring the surprised looks of the well-heeled clientele and the obvious horror of the door staff, who believed their job was to keep the undesirable elements of Lahore society outside in order to protect those who lived in the luxury world of the rich from embarrassment. The restaurant owner was keen not to be seen as the man who turned children away from his doors if they were in the company of a man like Ehsan Khan.

When their orders had been taken, the staff drew back and the two of them were alone. Iqbal took a long drink of his water. As well as being hungry, he was also starting to feel deeply battered. His legs were throbbing from being dragged behind the truck the previous night, his ribs were stabbing and now the whole side of his face was stinging from the most recent blow, making his ears ring. Despite everything, however, he felt that good manners demanded he should make polite conversation with his eating companion.

'Fatima says you went to prison,' he opened the conversation with a question he'd been wanting to ask for some time. 'Is it true?'

'Yes,' Ehsan nodded. 'A few times.'

'Did they torture you?' Iqbal knew that most prisoners had to expect to suffer torture if they fell into the hands of the police.

'I don't like to talk about it.'

'Why not?'

Ehsan sighed. 'Because that's why they do it.'

'What do you mean?'

'They torture people so that when they come out they will tell everyone how terrible it was and so everyone will be scared of the police and less willing to do what is right, just in case they are arrested.'

Iqbal fell silent for a few moments, thinking through Ehsan's words.

'But they shouldn't torture people,' he said eventually, 'and if you don't tell people then no one will ever make them stop.'

Ehsan narrowed his eyes and stared hard at the boy. 'Complicated, isn't it?' he said.

Iqbal nodded. 'So, what did they arrest you for?'

'I was working as a journalist and I asked questions that they didn't want to answer. The government of this country doesn't like people asking questions.'

'The owner of the brick kiln said you were a spy working for the Jews or the Indians. Is that true?'

'Of course not.' Ehsan sounded mildly irritated. 'They say that to turn public opinion against us. They say we're trying to wreck the Pakistani economy by forcing up wages and removing the child workforce. But what use is an economy that requires so many people to remain penniless slaves all their lives?'

Ehsan had noticed that the restaurant staff, who had been manning the desk by the door to make sure no undesirables got in, were becoming agitated by something that was happening outside. From the way they kept glancing across at their table he guessed it was something to do with them. He decided to ignore it in the hope that he could at least eat his meal before anything else happened.

As he brought the food over, the head waiter bent his mouth close to Ehsan's ear. 'There seems to be a crowd gathering on the steps, Mr Khan. It might be an idea if you had a word with them before the police arrive and start to cause trouble.'

Ehsan nodded his understanding, but didn't stand up immediately. He took a few mouthfuls of bread and chewed thoughtfully for a moment, staring hard at Iqbal.

'What is it?' Iqbal asked, but Ehsan didn't answer.

After what seemed like an eternity to Iqbal, and to the restaurant management, Ehsan stood up and held out his hand for the boy to come with him. Iqbal took the proffered hand and walked to the door without asking any more questions. He was startled as they got closer to see there was a crowd of children outside staring in through the glass. They seemed to have filled the whole square. He recognised some of them as the brick kiln children.

When Ehsan threw open the door and walked out, with Iqbal in tow, a cheer went up and many of the children punched the air in excitement. Iqbal's brow was as furrowed as an old man's as he tried to work out what was going on. Who were they cheering? He looked around but could see no one of importance waving to the crowd. They were all looking in his direction and he wondered if he should cheer too, even though he didn't know what it was for.

Ehsan let go of his hand and raised both of his arms in the air to quieten the crowd, but it was several minutes before they were hushed enough to hear what he had to say. Iqbal stared up at him proudly, and joined in the applause, realising it was Ehsan they had all come to see.

'You're right,' Ehsan said, his voice ringing round the square like a politician at a rally, 'to come here to praise Iqbal. You're right to want to shake him by the hand.'

The furrows on Iqbal's brow deepened again and he stopped clapping as he heard these words. Ehsan was saying the crowd were there to see him, but he couldn't understand why. Ehsan must have got it wrong. He felt embarrassed for him and wondered if he could just sneak back into the restaurant and leave Ehsan with his admirers.

'But what you must do is follow his example,' Ehsan went on and Iqbal noticed that many in the crowd were nodding their agreement. 'Iqbal was a slave, just like many of you, but he had the strength to fight back, to refuse to let anyone take away his freedom. Now he's getting an education so he can help other people like himself. That is what you must all do. You must learn to read and write, to add up numbers, so you can get proper jobs and no one can make you their slaves again. Iqbal is a hero, and you can all be heroes too.'

He pointed to the small, confused boy standing beside him to direct their applause towards him. As the sound of the cheering and clapping swelled again, bouncing off the surrounding buildings, Iqbal's brow cleared and his face broke into a beaming smile. They really were applauding him. They thought he had done something good! Now Ehsan would have to allow him to go on other missions, because he'd done well.

'We are free!' he shouted, throwing his arms in the air. 'We are free!'

The children nearest the front picked up the chant and it spread backwards through the crowd like the roar of a steam engine gathering speed. Ehsan spotted the police vans drawing up at the back of the crowd before anyone else and put his arm around Iqbal's shoulders, guiding him quickly down the steps and through the arch towards the park.

Iqbal tried to shake the many hands that were stretched out towards him but Ehsan told him to hurry. The sounds of anger and panic were spreading forwards through the crowd almost as quickly as the chanting had travelled the other way as the police waded in with guns and batons, hitting indiscriminately as they went, dragging anyone who didn't run away fast enough into the vans. As soon as each van was filled to capacity and they could force no more bodies in through the doors, they slammed them shut and drove to the police station to unload them. Within five minutes the crowd and the police had vanished and the waiters were clearing away the uneaten food from Ehsan and Iqbal's table. It was as if the whole event had never happened.

'Why did they all gather like that?' Iqbal asked as they hurried through the streets towards the sanctuary of the Freedom Campus.

'They heard what you did last night and they wanted to see what you look like,' Ehsan said, as if it was obvious.

'How did they find out?'

'There aren't many people in this country willing to help people like them. When someone steps forward the news travels fast. You've become a hero.'

'A hero?'

'It's a big responsibility,' Ehsan said, 'especially when you still haven't had any lunch.'

CHAPTER ELEVEN

POISONED WORDS

Every waking moment of Ehsan's life was taken up with BLLF business, and many of his restless sleeping hours were filled with nightmares about the children he'd not yet been able to reach. Iqbal found himself doing the same. Both of them found it impossible to interest themselves in other things as long as they knew there were still children being held as slaves, exploited, tortured, raped and even killed upon the whims of their owners.

Not every child with a job in Pakistan was being treated badly; many were happy to be working a few hours a day and earning money to help their families. It was hard to explain to those who had never visited one of the worst factories just how bad things could be. But they both worked at it, going over the same conversation dozens of times a day with anyone who would listen, demanding to be believed.

It was impossible to ascertain accurately how many children there were in the world living in the worst conditions, but even the most conservative estimates made by charities put the figure at millions. When Ehsan had told him that, Iqbal had made him write the number out, so that he could see how many noughts it had. He had tried to imagine how many people that might be, but the scale of it all made him feel sick and he had to stop. It was simply too big a problem for him to comprehend, so he tried to concentrate his thoughts on the children in the individual factories that he saw or heard about, so that he didn't become overwhelmed. But it was impossible to keep his mind from wandering sometimes and his whole face would crease up with concern.

When he had been working in the carpet factory himself, he'd often worried about the other children, wondering how they would ever be able to escape when they sometimes couldn't even remember where they'd come from.

'How will you find all these families?' he had asked Ehsan the day after the children from his own factory had been released.

'We follow up any clues they can give us,' Ehsan said, 'but if that fails we try to find a new family for them. Sometimes we just have to look after them until they're old enough to leave school and get proper jobs.'

'What happens if they don't want to go back to their families, like me?'

'We try to do the best for everyone,' Ehsan said, 'but sometimes it isn't possible.'

'I've been lucky, haven't I?'

'You were lucky to be born a little different to other people,' Ehsan said, smiling at the look of puzzlement on the boy's face. 'You have an intelligence beyond your years, and a humanity. That has raised you above the crowd.'

Now that Iqbal realised there were many hundreds of millions who were in the same, and possibly worse, conditions, he found himself lying awake at night worrying about all of them, feeling the crushing weight of so many people that he would never be able to do anything for. Having listened to Ehsan talking so much, it seemed obvious to him that it was the most important job in the world to save the slaves, and he couldn't understand how other people were able to go on with their normal lives, doing nothing to help.

His face grew as grave as Ehsan's, his brow always furrowed with concern as he struggled with the idea of how best to save the world. It wasn't just the children who still needed to be saved, they both also worried about the ones who'd been freed and were always in danger of being taken by force and put back to work. If a freed slave couldn't be found a place in a school and somewhere safe to live, it was never long before he or she was snatched back off the street, either by their old owner, or by someone else equally unscrupulous.

It was impossible to keep a watch on all of them and sometimes there would be reports from the schools of pupils who just stopped turning up and whose families denied all knowledge of their whereabouts. When there was so much to be done it was impossible ever to take time off or think about yourself.

The hours Iqbal spent with Mrs Malik in class, or with her and Fatima in their home after school, were the only ones that weren't taken up with the BLLF. If Ehsan was going to visit one of the other schools he would take Iqbal with him, watching proudly as his protégé sat amongst the children in some distant village, talking to them about the importance of education and begging them to work hard so that their own children would never have to go through what they had been through.

Now that he had proved himself to be so brave and determined, he was allowed to come on almost all the missions to free children from factories. Because he was small and seemed to be about their age, the children were less alarmed by his unexpected arrival in their midst than they were when adults like Ehsan appeared from nowhere. His calmness and seriousness often seemed to give them the confidence they needed to walk away from their oppressors. The situations Iqbal found himself in with the factory owners were often dangerous, but his confidence never seemed to falter. His faith in Ehsan and his utter conviction that they were doing the right thing somehow kept him safe. Sometimes one of the women in the organisation would chide Ehsan for allowing the boy to work so hard.

'Let him have some fun,' Mrs Baber would say. 'Let

him have some time off. He's too young to have the cares of the whole world on his shoulders.'

Whenever Ehsan suggested that he should have a day off to play, Iqbal would look completely puzzled.

'What for?' he'd ask, and Ehsan would know exactly what he meant, feeling the same himself.

'It's what boys do,' Ehsan said on one occasion.

'Not slave boys,' Iqbal replied.

For a terrible moment Ehsan wondered if he was guilty of turning Iqbal into a different sort of slave: a slave to his conscience. But now that the seeds he'd sown in the boy's mind had put down such firm roots, he wasn't sure how he could do anything to change him. Iqbal had made the decision to follow the path that Ehsan had showed him, and would not be dissuaded.

Many of the children in the schools had heard about Iqbal from their teachers, who would tell them stories of his daring raids on factories and his bravery in the face of owners with guns and clubs. Sometimes they would make up new stories to keep their listeners enthralled, crediting Iqbal with almost superhuman powers. These stories would be passed on as truth, increasing the awe in which he was held by those who'd never even met him. It became difficult to discern where the truth ended and the myths began. Even Iqbal would be confused sometimes, trying to remember whether he really had done something that was being talked about.

If the pupils knew he was coming to a school they would prepare songs and speeches for Iqbal, and he would sit for hours at a time, entranced by every child who stood up and recited, applauding madly after each shy performance, as if he'd just witnessed the greatest piece of professional artistry. He thought that being a teacher must be the most rewarding of jobs.

If he was aware these children looked on him as a living hero, he didn't show it. The intensity of his stare and the urgency of his words as he spoke about the future of Pakistan gave the impression he had no self-awareness at all, that his whole being was taken up with mastering the problems of child labour and education.

Teachers who never knew when their next pay-day might be, who laboured every day to lift the damaged children in their care towards some sort of enlightenment, were heartened by his visits. He gave them hope that if they managed to find only one or two children like him in their careers they would still have done a worthwhile job and moved the cause forward.

He and Ehsan would always stay longer than expected on these visits, sitting in hidden backstreet courtyards, which had been converted into schools by the families who lived there, or under trees or canopies in open spaces, listening to the lessons and telling the children of their dreams for the future.

The wounds Iqbal had received during his first raid had

healed slowly, but he never mentioned the pains that lingered as his ribs repaired themselves and the bruising in his neck diminished. He didn't want Ehsan to think he was anything other than completely fit, otherwise he might refuse to allow him to come on any more raids. When you've been in pain all your life you learn to ignore it and concentrate on other things.

After Iqbal had been living in Lahore for nearly a year Ehsan become concerned by his small stature. Even now he was eating properly, he still didn't seem to be growing as other boys his age did. He took him to see a doctor, who said that the damage had probably been done in his early years.

'If you crush a living thing into a small space, keep it in the dark, restrict its movements, then it will not flourish,' the doctor explained. 'His joints were not exercised properly as a small child and his body was not nourished with a proper diet. But many boys grow later in their teens. I wouldn't worry.'

Ehsan was willing to take that explanation for the moment, not knowing who else to ask, but his mind still wasn't settled. He didn't mention it again because he could see it didn't bother Iqbal and he didn't want to make him self-conscious. He had always tried to keep a distance between himself and the children he rescued. There were simply too many of them for him to hope to maintain a relationship with them once they'd been freed and found a safe place to stay. But Iqbal was beginning to feel like a son to him, someone he could teach and mould to become exactly like himself, the vain dream of most parents.

Ehsan often worried what would become of the BLLF if anything happened to himself. Someone could decide that he had become too much of a nuisance and could arrange to end his life any day; or he could find a charge had been trumped up that would put him in jail for years. Who would take over the running of the organisation then?

So many of the people who gave most generously of their time were bonded labourers he'd freed over the years. They might have grown up to be willing workers for the cause, but the experiences they'd endured as children nearly always left them unable to stand up to authority in the way he was able to. They usually had endless reserves of patience, which meant they never gave up on the cause, but they lacked the confidence to make their point when necessary. Iqbal was the exception. Slavery seemed to have added steel to his soul rather than damaged it.

Most weeks they travelled out of the city to addresses that had been brought to them with stories of cruelty and abuse. Sometimes they would free a dozen or more children at a time, and sometimes the missions would fail and they would be chased off by the owners before they'd been able to build the confidence of the children enough to persuade them to follow.

Whenever they came back to Lahore empty-handed Iqbal would sink into a dark mood for several hours, knowing that those children would be made to pay the next day for the disturbed sleep of the owner; that they would be made to work longer and harder to compensate for the disruption. Even if the slaves had refused to go they would still have been blamed for the inconvenience and disruption. The people who ran these factories and workplaces relied on those they employed believing there was no one else for them to turn to, that there was no hope of any sort of a better life. It was the only way to keep them obedient and productive. If people like Iqbal whispered in their ears, spreading ideas of freedom and education, it was all the harder for the owners to keep control without increasing the threats and the violence.

Sometimes he would travel with Ehsan to demonstrate in public places, just like on the day they first met. He enjoyed those outings, spending the days before helping to make posters and flags. At the meetings he would wave banners and shout, 'We are free!' at the top of his voice.

Not every raid on a factory happened in the night; sometimes he would walk into the workshops in broad daylight and talk to the children as they worked, taking advantage of the owner being away and the overseers being too craven to protest at the invasion of their fiefdoms.

'You should come with me,' he'd tell the children. 'I'm free and you can be the same. They can't stop you. Just stand up and walk out. It's illegal for them to keep you here.'

Not all the children had the courage to take up his offer, but many did and he would lead them to Ehsan and the lawyers, who would visit their families and argue their cases for them. If they couldn't stay with their families then they would come back to the Freedom Campus in Lahore, just as Iqbal had done, before being found somewhere else safe to stay.

Iqbal had moved out of the Freedom Campus into a flat just across the road with several other BLLF workers. Ehsan sometimes stayed there when he was in town and every room was full of boxes of leaflets, broken office equipment that somebody was hoping to get mended, and makeshift beds.

Sometimes the owners would succeed in grabbing the children back from the BLLF. There were always times when there would be no one watching them. They might be on their way to the courthouse, or going from their schools to wherever they were staying, when the owners and their thugs would appear from doorways and snatch them back as easily as rats might lift fledglings that strayed too far from the protection of their nests.

The families of the children were also vulnerable to pressure from owners who insisted that Ehsan was lying, and that their debts still stood. If a worker had been stolen from a factory, the owner would reason, then the debtor family must provide him with a replacement or repay the loan. Since none of these families had any money, the escape of one child could then lead to the imprisonment of another. Usually not being able to read, the families would be unable to use the literature that Ehsan and his co-workers distributed and they were soon out-argued by stronger and more ruthless opponents.

'Why doesn't the government send the police and the army in to save slave children?' Iqbal asked Ehsan one day when they were driving back after an abortive mission.

'Because they believe it's the way things are and there's nothing they can do about it,' Ehsan shrugged. 'I've spoken to government ministers who just tell me child labour is a tradition in Pakistan, and that the economy is dependent on it. They tell me to be patient and that eventually the economy will develop as it has in other countries and people will no longer need to hire children to do the work of adults.'

'Does it happen in other countries?'

'It happens wherever there's poverty. It used to happen in the West but they became prosperous and educated and able to defend their children. But it took a long time to change people's attitudes. Even ministers who believe it's wrong to make children work in factories will have them working in their homes as servants and will think nothing of it. They won't give it a second thought, and when you point it out they'll say there's no comparison, that they are kind employers and that the children are happy to be working in nice conditions. Every day they go out on the streets and they're surrounded by children who are working every waking hour, serving tea, begging, working in shops, in restaurants, but they don't notice them, any more than they would notice leaves on a tree. It's just "the way things are".'

Their discussions would go on for hours sometimes as Iqbal struggled against the realisation that he was fighting an impossible fight; that he would never be able to win. The truth was that he would have to be satisfied with the small victories and the individual successes of the children who made something of their lives after he had played a part in their rescue, because he would never be able to abolish slavery like President Lincoln had in America.

'The Americans may have abolished the formal business of slavery on the plantations in the south,' Ehsan explained during another of their conversations, 'but they went on using children in factories for many years after that. It wasn't considered slavery, it was considered "necessity".'

Iqbal was learning so much so quickly his brain never stopped buzzing. Mrs Malik was amazed by how quickly he'd started to read and write. It was as if the knowledge had always been locked inside him and he'd just been waiting for a key to release it. Every time he made another leap forward he would rush to show Ehsan after school. He wished he could go back to Muridke and show his mother how well he was doing; perhaps he could even persuade his brother, Patras, to come to Lahore and join in with the schooling. But his courage would fail at the thought of actually going back. He was afraid that someone would grab him and deliver him back to the carpet master.

He was still woken in the night from time to time by nightmares in which he was spinning upside down in the dark. He would see the faces of his fellow workers in the carpet factory, sometimes mixed up with children he had rescued since. There were always grown men's voices shouting at him and sticks raised, ready to fall. He would return to consciousness bathed in sweat and panting with panic and it would sometimes take a long time to calm his heart down enough to allow sleep to return.

The thrill of suddenly being able to see sense in words that had previously been no more than abstract patterns grew almost too intense to bear when he received his first letter. It was delivered by hand to the BLLF office some time during the night, and was waiting on the desk for him when he finished school the next day and walked over to look for Ehsan as usual.

'This is for you,' Mrs Baber said, flicking the envelope in his direction. 'It seems your fame is spreading.'

He didn't open it for a few moments, wanting to savour the feeling of anticipation for as long as he could bear it. Mrs Baber was watching him out of the corner of her eye as she talked to two other women Iqbal didn't know. Eventually he couldn't stand the suspense for a moment longer and carefully peeled open the envelope, pulling out the piece of cheap writing paper folded inside. He opened it up and squinted at the few words written in an ugly scrawl.

'Leave our children alone,' the message read, 'or you will die.'

He read it several times, to make sure he'd grasped its meaning fully. They were all words he understood and he was confident he'd read them right, but he couldn't believe someone had actually addressed them to him. He checked the envelope again and it was definitely his name. Mrs Baber noticed his hand shaking and came over to sit beside him. For a moment he tried to hide the letter but when he felt her warm, plump hand on his he relented and passed it to her. She made some loud sucking noises with her teeth as she read it.

'The world is full of ignorant people, Iqbal,' she said, putting her arm around his trembling shoulders. 'You're going to have to be very strong. No child should have to face the things that you're facing. Ehsan should not expose you to such things so young.'

When Ehsan saw the letter he shook his head in

despair. He'd received many dozens of such messages in his career but they still had the power to make his blood chill. When someone came up to him at a rally and shouted abuse, or even hit him, it somehow wasn't as threatening as this sort of anonymous threat, where you had no idea who the enemy was. There was no way to assess the danger they might pose and take appropriate evasive action; they might be simply fools and cowards, or they could be people with a serious intent to silence their targets.

'People who write these letters are cowards,' he said to Iqbal. 'They're people who do not have the courage to tell you what they think of you face to face. They never do any more than this.'

'Okay,' Iqbal said, wanting to believe his friend but also wanting to know who would ever have written him such a message.

'Words can be a very powerful weapon,' Ehsan went on. 'By scribbling those few words on a piece of paper this man has struck more fear into your heart than if he'd attacked you with a club. So you must remember what they are.' He screwed the piece of paper up in one hand and tossed it aside. 'They're just words on paper. They can't hurt you. If you hadn't learned to read you wouldn't know they existed and they would no longer have any power.'

Three nights later the BLLF office came under attack. No one knew anything about it until Mrs Baber came in the next morning to open up and found the door swinging off its hinges. The corpse of a dog was hanging from the ceiling fan and the walls had been daubed with its blood. Some of the writing was hard to make out but the words 'death', 'traitors' and 'Indian spies' were just visible amid the angry smears.

No one felt like going to the police. It would only mean more trouble and someone would have to find the money for a bribe if they arrested the wrong person and he had to be rescued from the police station. What could the police do, anyway?

Ehsan's eyes looked even sadder than usual when he surveyed the damage later that morning.

'What will we do now?' Iqbal asked that afternoon, after school.

'We'll wash the walls and keep doing exactly the same things,' Ehsan replied. 'We have to. There's no choice. They're only attacking us because we're being successful and worrying them. If we have to put them out of business in order to force them to treat their workers fairly, then they're bound to be angry and to want to stop us. But still, we must be careful, because there are people out there who wish us harm.'

'I don't understand why they hate us so much,' Iqbal said. 'We're only trying to do the right thing.'

'It's because they believe we're threatening their liveli-hoods and their way of life,' Ehsan replied. 'They can't believe there's a better way of doing things. They're not brave people and they feel threatened. If they just travelled to countries in Europe or to America and saw what can be achieved when you embrace progress and change they would be amazed, but these people would never allow their eyes to be opened in that way. They are the sort of people who never move out of their own villages, who like to stay in places where they believe they are important, or where they hold power by being physically stronger than those around them.'

Iqbal knew he was right. If they gave up their struggle then nothing would ever change, but he didn't like the idea that there were now people who wished him dead. He wasn't frightened of death, he believed he'd endured worse at the hands of his former owner, but the idea of there being so much hatred in the world that it could spill over onto people who were doing nothing more than trying to help children, left him deeply sad and troubled.

'Why don't you ever smile?' Fatima asked Iqbal one evening when they'd grown tired of playing badminton and were sitting down together for a rest.

'Don't I?' Iqbal was startled to discover that was her view. One of the things he liked best about her was the ease with which she showed her dazzling white teeth when anything pleased her.

'You frown all the time,' she ran her finger along one

of the furrows on his brow to prove her point. Her gentle touch made him smile. 'There you are,' she clapped her hands happily. 'You're quite handsome when you do that.'

Iqbal felt himself blushing and looked away. They were quiet for a few moments.

'You can't carry the weight of the whole world on your shoulders,' Fatima broke the silence. 'Some things just can't be changed.'

'If I thought that then I would give up on life,' Iqbal said. 'We have to change what we know to be wrong.'

'I'm going to be travelling out to Muridke,' Ehsan told him one day. 'Would you like to visit your family?'

Iqbal felt a tremor of fear run through him, making him feel sick.

'You don't have to,' Ehsan said, 'but I think it would be quite safe now, and I'm sure your mother would like to see you. Your father and the other men will have heard stories of what you have done. They won't expect to be able to control you any more.'

'Will you be there?' Iqbal asked. 'All the time?'

'If you want,' Ehsan ruffled his hair. 'Whatever makes you comfortable.'

Iqbal thought for a moment. 'All right then.'

The next day the two of them caught a bus out of town. Iqbal was always impressed by how calmly Ehsan endured the heat and discomfort of public transport. When Ehsan had first started taking him around Lahore on buses Iqbal had been surprised. He'd imagined that someone of his mentor's stature would always travel everywhere by car.

'No,' Ehsan had smiled, 'I don't have the money for a car. I rely on the goodwill of others to lend them to me when I need them. Most of the time I travel like everyone else.'

They walked from the main road down to the village, where Ehsan stopped on the way to visit a school. Iqbal sat with him amongst the pupils and tried to concentrate, but his mind kept wandering back to the meeting that was about to take place. Ehsan, as always, seemed in no hurry to leave the teachers and the children but eventually they said their goodbyes and continued on their way. The usual crowd of children attached themselves as they came into the village, one or two of them plucking up the courage to ask for money. Ehsan ignored them and they didn't pester. He had an air about him that discouraged people from invading his space.

When they reached Iqbal's family house he rapped smartly on the door. There was a long pause before it creaked open and Sobya's nervous face appeared in the crack. A surge of affection brought tears to Iqbal's eyes as he saw how pretty she had become. In the time since he had last seen her she had grown and begun to show signs of turning into a woman. He was relieved to see that she was still at home and not working in a factory. For a second her eyes connected with Iqbal's and he knew she was just as surprised by the changes she saw in him, before she lowered her eyes modestly.

'Is Inayat Bibi in?' Ehsan asked.

'Yes,' Sobya nodded, opening the door wide enough for them to step into the courtyard.

'Who is it?' Inayat demanded from the kitchen, quickly pulling her scarf up over her hair when she saw Ehsan.

'Your son has come to visit you,' Ehsan said.

'My baby!' Inayat put her arms around Iqbal. 'You have grown into such a young man.'

Over the next hour she fussed around them as if they were honoured guests, chiding them for not giving her enough warning to prepare a meal and insisting that they had cold drinks. Iqbal studied his mother as she jumped up and down to wait on them, her eyes always avoiding his stare. He felt a strange feeling, a mixture of love and pity. Now that he had met so many children from homes very like his he looked on his mother in a different way. He realised that no mothers wanted to give their children away, but that often they had no choice. He wished she would stop trying so hard to impress Ehsan. To distract himself from these thoughts he tried to imagine what she must have been like when she was Sobya's age, before she married Saif and life became so hard. Sobya hovered by the door, unsure whether she wanted to come in or not, enjoying being in her brother's company, even if only for a short while.

When they eventually stood to leave, Inayat asked Ehsan if there was any chance of more money to make up for the fact that Iqbal was not contributing to the family income.

'He is a young man now,' she argued, 'he would be bringing in money to help support his sister if he still lived in Muridke. Sobya needs so many things now she is getting older, and now my son is working for you.' There was a hint of accusation in her voice.

'Iqbal isn't working for me,' Ehsan insisted, 'he's studying at school and helping to free the children when he can. He has no money. And if he had not escaped from the carpet factory he would still be working off his supposed debt. But I will arrange for some more to be brought to you from BLLF funds, to help you take care of Sobya.'

'Thank you, thank you,' she said, bowing her head and pressing the palms of her hands together.

Once they were back on the bus to Lahore, Iqbal found he was able to breathe easily again. Even with Ehsan to protect him he was still uncomfortable being in Muridke, half expecting the carpet master to pounce from a backstreet and drag him away for punishment.

'My sister is going to be a woman soon, isn't she?' he said after a while.

'She is,' Ehsan agreed. 'And a very pretty one too.'

'You were right,' Iqbal went on after a while. 'Coming here was a good thing to do. I would like to come and see them again soon.'

'Whenever you want,' Ehsan said. 'Maybe one day you'll even feel able to come on your own.'

'I'm not sure I feel quite ready for that yet,' Iqbal said.

He would have liked to think he wasn't afraid of anything any more, but so many memories of pain and fear didn't disappear simply because you want them to.

CHAPTER TWELVE

A MEETING IN VIENNA

Ehsan always felt a little lost whenever he left Pakistan. Travelling abroad was exciting and it was wonderful to see how it was possible for people to live in countries relatively free of bullying and corruption, but he could never pretend he was quite comfortable anywhere but his homeland. However much he wanted to change things, he loved Pakistan and always looked forward to returning to the place where there was still so much for him to do.

Some travellers seemed to flourish on schedules packed with airports and hotel rooms, growing used to ordering room service meals, waiting to board planes and living out of suitcases, but he could never adapt to it all with any ease. Trips were necessary adventures if he wanted to spread the word and get international help, but they were seldom a pleasure for him.

Wherever he went in the world he would always wear the same traditional Pakistani clothes that he wore at home in Lahore: the long billowing white shirt and loose trousers, and then waistcoats and jackets if the weather was inclement, which it seemed to be most of the time in Europe, as far as he could make out. He cut a conspicuous figure striding around the streets of foreign cities, proud of his nationality and his country's customs and traditions – at least some of them. Other men might have adapted their wardrobe to a more westernised style, but he was never happy with compromises. New clothes would have cost too much money anyway, money that was always needed for fighting the cause.

He missed the heat whenever he was away from it. Not that he would have had any idea what the weather was like from the windowless basement of the conference hall in Vienna, where he was manning the BLLF stall. The conference going on above was on human rights, and hundreds of organisations like the BLLF had booked stands in order to tell their stories to the crowds who came to listen.

To a man like Doug Cahn from the Reebok Human Rights Foundation, who'd flown in from America for the conference, that giant basement was a confusing bazaar, filled with thousands of different images of horror. Every stand told a different tale of abuse and cruelty. Every person Doug spoke to and every leaflet he picked up or poster his eyes rested on cried out on behalf of different oppressed people who were unable to make anyone hear their pleas for help.

As he walked around the crowded aisles he felt an overwhelming sense of helplessness in the face of so much unfairness and suffering, so much cruelty and torture. How was it possible to choose one cause over another when every one of them seemed so urgent and so pitiful? But that was what he had to do; he must find people who would be worthy beneficiaries of the Reebok Human Rights Awards.

As he reached the BLLF booth Doug paused for a second, caught by an image of a child in a poster. In those few seconds Ehsan pounced and introduced himself. Ehsan was always desperate to speak about the BLLF to anyone who stood still long enough to listen. A shy man in many ways, he was never backward in talking about the subject that filled his every waking moment.

Doug smiled his encouragement to the sad-faced man standing in front of him.

'This truly is a hall or horrors,' he said.

Ehsan nodded, and having caught the passer-by's attention proceeded to explain what his organisation did, as he always did to everyone he met.

'Please,' he said, giving Doug a flyer, 'we're holding a seminar upstairs later this afternoon. Come and listen and I'll be explaining more.'

Doug thanked him, took the flyer and moved on.

Later that day, from his vantage point on the platform, Ehsan was pleased to see the American had taken up his invitation and had joined the audience. After some introductory remarks by a chairman, Ehsan stood up to address the room.

'I want to talk about one particular child,' he said, his voice only just loud enough for everyone in the room to hear, making them crane forward and concentrate. 'His name is Iqbal Masih and I have only known him for eighteen months.'

He proceeded to tell the tale of how he'd found Iqbal at one of his rallies, how the boy had blossomed the moment he was exposed to education and how he had taken the cause of freeing other children as his own. The room was silent as they all listened. Ehsan was able to talk from the heart in a way few of the other speakers had been able to do. He could picture his young friend as clearly as if he was in the room with them, with his earnest expression and determination to help other children like himself, and was able to convey the same picture to the assembled audience.

When he finally sat down to applause a number of people had questions, none of which were new to him, all of which gave him opportunities to paint a more vivid picture of the hundreds of thousands of slaves still at work in Pakistan, and the millions more in other countries. Figures that seemed so familiar to him, still had the power to shock those who had not registered the enormity of the problem.

When he finally returned to his booth in the basement he found Doug Cahn already there, waiting for him, looking thoughtful.

'That was a great talk,' the American said.

'Thank you,' Ehsan replied, not sure what else to say, conscious that his visitor had something on his mind and was looking for a way to phrase it.

'You know, we provide Reebok Human Rights Awards to young people who have made substantial contributions to human rights in non-violent ways. It seems to me that your young man could some day be a worthy applicant. If he were to win an award it would help to promote the issue of child bondage in the US, don't you think? It's not a subject the public knows a whole lot about.'

'The sports goods industry has traditionally been one of the biggest employers of bonded labour in the third world,' Ehsan said quietly.

'We're very aware of that,' Doug said. 'That's why Reebok is so anxious to distance ourselves from those sorts of practices, and we want to help repair the damage that companies in our industry might have done in the past. We have a football factory in Pakistan and we insist that no children are employed there, and that none of the work is sent out to other factories where children are employed. We feel very strongly about it.'

'Good,' Ehsan smiled and nodded his approval. If only more companies took that approach his work would be a lot easier. He noticed that some other people were passing by behind the American; he was nervous about missing the opportunity to talk to them if he spent too long with one person.

'The award would be worth $15,000 to him,' Doug went on, unsure if he had Ehsan's full attention, 'and would provide a good platform for your organisation to speak from.'

Ehsan blinked, several times, as he took in the information.

'That would be more money than he could imagine,' he said.

'Can we stay in touch over this?' Doug asked, passing Ehsan his card. 'I really think he sounds like a worthy recipient.'

'We can certainly talk about it,' Ehsan said, cautiously. He met so many people on his travels who were moved by what he had to say and promised to help. Some of them tried, but many became distracted by other priorities in their own lives and soon forgot the promises they'd made at a moment when their emotions were engaged. Ehsan had learned never to build his hopes up prematurely. America was a long way away from Pakistan in so many ways and the administration of such an award would be bound to be complicated. He wasn't going to be rude, but he would believe it when he saw it.

Once he was back in Lahore the chaos of his daily life

immediately swallowed any good intentions he might have had for following up leads he'd made during the conference. There were always people talking to him and phone calls to be made, new children to be looked after. Letters were delivered, always urgent, along with legal papers. The faxes that arrived from Reebok from time to time were relegated to piles awaiting attention.

Everywhere that Ehsan went these piles of paper grew and gathered dust: at the BLLF office, at the Freedom Campus and at the flat where he had a room to sleep in. Once any piece of paper had been covered by later arrivals there was seldom any chance it would rise to the surface again. Doug's faxes disappeared in the bustle of communication.

But Doug wasn't a man to give up easily. The fact that Ehsan wasn't greedy for the award seemed to confirm that he was a man of integrity, with other things on his mind. He persevered and over the following months some of his communications made it through. The two men began to correspond erratically, slowly building up a bond of mutual trust. Doug learned more about BLLF and Iqbal, and Ehsan reassured himself that Reebok were sincere in their wish to help the cause.

When he realised that Doug was not going to be one of the many people who made promises and then forgot them, Ehsan looked more closely at what was being offered. The more he thought about it the more he could see just what a good opportunity it would be for both Iqbal and the BLLF. Iqbal would get to travel to America and enjoy experiences that most small boys can only dream of, and the story of the tens of thousands of children working in Pakistan as bonded labourers would reach a huge number of new people. He'd always been frustrated by his inability to inform people in Europe and America that when they bought cheap goods from the Third World the people who were suffering were the slaves who were forced to produce them for no money. Pakistan was such a distant concept for most westerners, but Reebok was a powerful company and would be able to get the message to a lot of people.

Ehsan suggested an alternative plan to Reebok, that they should award some money to the BLLF as well as giving Iqbal his prize. He wanted to test the company's intentions and be sure they had the long-term interests of slave children at heart, not just the short-term advantages of attaching their name to a young hero. Once he was certain the company was sincere in its offer, and he had spent many hours weighing up all the pros and cons, Ehsan decided it was time to explain to Iqbal what was happening.

Knowing the boy had gone home with Mrs Malik after school as usual, Ehsan made his way to her house, after slipping a battered old map of the world into his pocket.

Iqbal and Fatima were sitting at the table in the open-fronted downstairs room, their eyes fixed on the cartoons flickering on the television screen. They both greeted Ehsan politely, but were far more interested in the television. Mrs Malik settled him at the table and brought him a cup of tea. Ehsan waited quietly until the cartoon was over, sipping his tea and dabbing his moustache dry after each sip. Mrs Malik went about her normal chores, not bothering him with conversation. She saw that he had important things on his mind.

Once the show was over and the children's attention had returned to the real world, Ehsan brought the map out of his pocket and spread it on the table without saying a word, as if absorbed in some private study. Fatima averted her eyes politely but Iqbal couldn't hide his curiosity for even a second. Pulling his legs up so he was kneeling on his chair he leant across to look at the map.

'If this is the whole world,' Ehsan said, 'and the blue is the sea which separates the countries, where do you suppose Pakistan is?'

Iqbal squinted hard at the different colours, trying to make out the words, most of which were completely unfamiliar. Fatima, seeing that her mother had moved away from the sink to look over their shoulders, decided it was all right for her to join in the game. They both searched as Ehsan sat back with folded arms and watched, expressionless. After a number of false starts they found the country, even managing to locate Lahore.

'And where do you think America is?' Ehsan asked.

Iqbal was practically climbing on the table in his excitement now at this new game and new opportunity to soak up fresh knowledge. America did not take as long to find as Pakistan.

'And a city called Boston?'

Once Iqbal's finger was firmly placed on Boston, Ehsan leant forward. 'You have been invited to go there to receive a Human Rights Award.'

Iqbal said nothing and frowned hard, trying to work out what this unexpected announcement meant. It didn't make sense. He decided to concentrate on one piece of it at a time.

'I'm going to America?'

'If you'd like to.'

'Who'll take me?'

'I'll take you.'

Iqbal nodded as if this was satisfactory. He now couldn't remember what the other bit of the announcement was.

'Why have I been invited there?'

'A big company, called Reebok …'

'Reebok?' Fatima forgot herself in her excitement at the sound of such a fashionable name. 'They make cool trainers, Iqbal. Really cool.'

'Shh, Fatima,' Mrs Malik put her finger to her lips to remind her daughter of her manners.

'Is that right, Fatima?' Ehsan laughed. 'There you are, Iqbal. Fatima approves.'

Fatima blushed and smiled shyly as Ehsan went on to explain why they wanted to give Iqbal the award.

'But I'm just trying to do what is right,' Iqbal said eventually. 'That's all.'

'Well, that is more than most people do,' Ehsan told him. 'So they want to recognise that achievement. They want to draw other people's attention to things you do in the hope that some others might decide to do something similar themselves.'

'I see.' That made more sense to him.

'Would you like to go?'

'If it's not too much trouble for you,' Iqbal said. 'I know how busy you are.'

'I think we could fit it in,' Ehsan said.

'You're going to America!' Fatima was unable to suppress her awe a moment longer. 'That will be so cool.'

'On the way we'll be stopping off here,' Ehsan said, leaning forward over the map again and placing his finger on Sweden. 'We have many friends and supporters in Sweden, people who have been out here and worked with us, and who've helped raise support over there for the BLLF. They're organising a conference in Stockholm. So you could give a speech to a very big audience. Think you could do that?'

'Give a speech? About what?'

'About bonded labour and why it's a bad thing. Just like you do when we go to meetings around the country.

Tell them who you are and what happened to you.'

'Will they understand me in Sweden?'

'I'll interpret into English for you,' Ehsan laughed. 'You'll be representing all the millions of slave children around the world, speaking on their behalf, telling their story.'

'Yes,' Iqbal nodded. 'I'd like to do that. It would be cool.'

In fact, he couldn't begin to imagine what it would be like to travel outside Pakistan. Would the rest of the world be like the scenes he saw on television between the cartoons?

Chapter Thirteen

A Great International Adventure

Iqbal had often watched the kites being flown above Lahore; sometimes he'd even flown one himself with Fatima. They would stand together on the roof of her house, him holding the end of the string while she threw the kite up into the air, shouting instructions to him as he struggled to make it take flight. He'd often thought how wonderful it must be to be able to fly above the city; to dip and rise on the currents, looking down on all the people as they scurried around with their worries and responsibilities. Now he was travelling way above any kites, looking down on the lights of the city below, too far up to be able to make out individual people, or even individual cars.

Lahore looked far more organised from above than it did from street level. When you couldn't see the dirt and the people any more you could make out the patterns of the streets and squares. You could see what the planners must have had in mind when they first built it. He'd often noticed how beautiful the buildings were beneath the cracks and flaking plaster, behind the tangles of electricity and telephone wires, the weeds and the chaos of people's washing and other possessions.

His feet didn't touch the floor of the plane and the stewardesses treated him with such unexpected politeness and kindness he wanted to hug them. Beneath the steady roar of the engines everything was hushed, voices courteous and lighting muted as the staff went about their job of making everyone as comfortable as possible. Ehsan was already working, writing and reading on the little table that he'd folded down in front of him, while Iqbal stared around in wonder.

Ehsan had warned him it would be cold in Sweden, but he couldn't imagine what that meant. He'd seen pictures of Europeans and they always seemed to be wearing an awful lot of clothes, so he'd agreed to bring the jacket Ehsan had found for him on a local market stall. He was also wearing the new shoes Ehsan had bought; he liked them, even though they were already rubbing his feet and making them sore.

'Everyone wears shoes in Europe,' Ehsan had informed him. 'It's far too cold to go barefooted or to wear sandals.'

'Everyone?' Iqbal asked, trying to imagine such a thing. 'Even the children and the beggars?'

'Everyone,' Ehsan assured him.

They'd talked a lot about what he would say in his speech and he'd decided to bring a beating comb with him. All carpet workers had them to tighten the lines of wool, but they were also used to beat the children when they didn't work fast enough or didn't obey orders instantly.

'I could hold up the beating comb for them to see,' he had said when he was planning the speech with Ehsan. 'Then I could hold up a pen and say that this is what the children of Pakistan need to be holding, not the comb. Then they'll understand that we need education instead of slavery. Would that be effective?'

'That would be very effective,' Ehsan had said. 'And I think they would like to know a bit about what it was like to work in the factory; how many hours did you have to spend there? What did they give you to eat? What was it like inside?'

'The heat, you mean? And the dust?'

'Yes, all that.'

'Is that what this conference is for?'

'The conference is to raise awareness in Europe that slavery still exists. We have a lot of people over there who work with BLLF and other organisations, but most other people still don't realise what is going on. Someone like you can help the organisers to get people to listen.'

'Is that why people keep asking for cheap carpets, because they don't realise who is making them?'

'Yes,' Ehsan nodded. 'That's pretty much what the problem is.'

Ever since then, Iqbal had been practising what he was going to say in his head. He'd grown a lot more confident about speaking since that first day when Ehsan had invited him up onto the platform to talk about himself. Nothing he'd done since then, however, had prepared him for the moment when he walked out onto the stage in Stockholm and saw several thousand pairs of eyes staring up at him from the giant hall beyond.

But then, everything had seemed strange from the moment the plane landed in Sweden. Life there seemed so orderly and the people were so polite to one another. There was none of the pushing and shouting and sweating he was used to at home. The floors of the airport were as clean as any grand hotel and, to his amazement, the streets they drove through were equally well cared for. There were no crowds of people hanging around on street corners, staring into space or jabbering at one another. Anyone who was outside seemed to be walking with purpose in order to get somewhere. Everyone he saw was smartly dressed, with well-groomed hair, and – just as Ehsan had predicted – everyone was wearing proper shoes, as if they were going to work in an office. The air was fresh and sharp, making him shiver but at the same time making his lungs feel cleansed when he breathed it in.

The hotel room was bigger, cleaner and sweeter smelling than he would ever have thought possible and he couldn't believe how nice the staff were to him. No one seemed to look through him as if he wasn't there, like they did at home. No one shouted at him as if he was a stray dog.

It had never occurred to him when he was a small child that not everywhere smelled as strongly as Muridke or that in some parts of the world smoothly surfaced roads and pavements were considered normal. He wished he could take everyone from his family in an aeroplane to look at the world and see how clean and comfortable life could be, so they would understand that they didn't have to live the same way their parents and grandparents and great-grandparents had. He wanted everyone to understand they were free to improve their lives if they just wanted to.

He often thought about his mother and brothers and sister in Muridke and wondered what would happen to them. Would he be able to help them to escape from their current lives – endlessly struggling just to get enough food on the table? Would Sobya one day be forced to sell her children to a man like the carpet master? Would she have to spend every day of her life fighting to survive, becoming old before her time?

Being in a place like Sweden, he began to wonder if his fears about going back to the Muridke on his own were foolish. Everyone here seemed so safe and confident; no one seemed frightened of the police. Soon, he told himself, he would go home on his own so he could tell his mother all about his adventures. He wanted to make her gasp with wonder and glow with pride. He hadn't felt he could talk freely when Ehsan was there;

he could tell that the presence of a stranger made her nervous and embarrassed, too worried about being a good hostess to give her son as much attention as she wanted.

There were other speakers before him on the platform and he knew that some of them were talking in English and others in Swedish, even though he couldn't make out the words they were using. He waited his turn patiently, knowing that Ehsan would tell him when it was time to stand up and walk to the podium. He didn't feel as nervous as he had done on the first outings with Ehsan in Pakistan. He felt safe amongst these people, none of whom he knew anything about. In Pakistan he never knew what people were going to shout at him, or whether they would try to hit him or chase him off. Here he instinctively felt he was amongst friends, that they were already on his side, that they were interested in him and what he had to say. Now he was on the stage, sitting next to Ehsan while the audience fell quiet and other people said things. He waited calmly to be told it was his moment to speak.

'Iqbal Masih.'

His name penetrated clearly through the gabble of foreign words and he glanced at Ehsan, who nodded. Both of them stood up. Iqbal looked out at the sea of faces stretching all the way to the distant walls of the hall and felt a smile spread over his face. A murmur seemed to rise from the crowd, which suggested they liked what they saw and wanted to encourage him. He could only just see over the lectern that he'd been put behind, but he felt ten feet tall.

'My name is Iqbal Masih,' he said, as he'd rehearsed in his head a thousand times, 'and I worked as a child slave in a carpet factory.' He listened to the echo of Ehsan's translation before continuing, as he always did, to describe what his life had been like at the carpet factory.

He told them about the beatings and the long hours, how they were never paid because they never managed to work off their initial debt. He told them how the children had no chance of an education and often died young, prematurely aged, their backs bent from their years of labour. And he told them how he had escaped and joined the BLLF to try to save others.

At the end, aware that every person in the hall was barely breathing in their determination to catch every translated word that Ehsan uttered, he held up the beating comb and the pen and told them where he believed the future lay.

As his last words sunk in, the whole audience rose to its feet like a tidal wave, their hands above their heads as they applauded, many with tears in their eyes. Iqbal beamed back, raising his arms in the air like a victorious prizefighter, astounded that his words could have had such an effect on such a huge crowd. If so many people felt so strongly about ending slavery, how come it still went on? How was it possible that people like the carpet master could keep children in their prisons when all these people felt like this? These people were the Westerners he had been told were making slavery inevitable with their demands for cheap goods. If that was so, why were they cheering so loudly? It was all so puzzling.

While they were in Sweden, Ehsan decided to take advantage of Iqbal's temporary celebrity status, and get a second opinion from a doctor about his lack of height. He asked one of his Swedish fundraisers to make enquiries and was told who the best growth specialist would be. An appointment was made. The doctor was happy to make space in his day to see such a distinguished visitor.

Iqbal was impressed by the hushed efficiency of the doctor's surgery; so different to the heat and chaos of any medical establishment he'd ever visited in Lahore. There had been several occasions when he had accompanied Ehsan to visit freed slaves who needed treatment, or BLLF workers who had fallen foul of the police and had to go to hospital to have their broken bones mended. The doctor in Stockholm had new carpet on the floor and all the time in the world to talk to them. His nurse took Iqbal away and X-rayed his skeleton, missing nothing from his knees to his fingers. He liked the cleanness of it all, it made him feel safe and cared for.

The Swedish doctor agreed with his Pakistani colleague that the problem could have been created by the lack of nutrition and exercise in his early years. However, when Iqbal told him about his uncle, who had never grown much taller than a child, the doctor nodded thoughtfully.

'It may be there is a genetic element here as well,' he said. 'I think it would be well worthwhile Iqbal taking some growth hormones. I would say from the X-rays that he is still only around eleven or twelve years old, so there is still time for him to catch up on his growing. You need to take this treatment every day for the next few years, Iqbal.'

Ehsan translated and Iqbal nodded seriously.

'You mustn't miss any days,' the doctor warned.

Ehsan's fellow workers in Sweden promised they would send supplies of the drugs over to Lahore to him at regular intervals and Iqbal was touched to think that so many people were willing to go to so much trouble on his behalf. He hoped he would grow; otherwise they would all be very disappointed.

By the time they were on the plane to Boston Iqbal felt like an experienced traveller, knowing just what to do with the headphones, hot towels and meals the stewardesses gave him.

'I'm going to America to accept an award,' he'd told a curious Pakistani stranger at the airport. 'I'm not quite sure what it's for, but I'm going to get it just the same.'

'Just continue to be yourself,' Ehsan advised him as the plane approached its destination, 'the Americans will love you even more than the Europeans. They're a more out-going people.'

'I'll tell them you're like their Abraham Lincoln,' Iqbal said, remembering one of Mrs Malik's history lessons, 'freeing Pakistan's slaves like he freed America's.'

Ehsan smiled modestly. 'Well,' he said, 'that would be a very nice thing for you to say.'

'But it's true,' Iqbal insisted.

'Except that I'm not a president and I can't change the laws, I can only campaign.'

'But when they hear that they'll understand that it's wrong to buy cheap carpets made by slaves.'

Iqbal's attention was soon distracted as he tackled the headphones and controls on the arm of his seat.

The moment he emerged from the airport, Iqbal recognised America from the television. This, he realised, was the land that the cartoons must depict. The people, the cars, the houses – everything was the same as he and Fatima had watched. This, he decided, was a country he would like to get to know better.

If the Swedish people had been polite, the Americans were effusive. Everyone who set eyes on the diminutive Iqbal seemed to fall in love on the spot. None of them could contain their urge to tell him how 'cute' he was and, in the case of the women, to hug him tightly to them. Iqbal's initial surprise at such treatment soon turned to pleasure as he basked in the friendly attention. He couldn't understand how people as nice as this could ever have been the ones responsible for buying cheap carpets and keeping people like his former master in business. He felt sure that if he could just explain to them how much suffering their hunt for bargains was causing for children in the developing world, they would refuse to buy carpets made by slaves any more.

'Just remember,' Ehsan would murmur to him at regular intervals, 'none of this is personal. You are just a representative of all the slave children. They're saluting all their courage, not just yours.'

'I know,' Iqbal would reply, a little exasperated that his friend would think he would become big-headed. 'I'm trying to remember everything to tell the others all about it when we get back.'

Slightly dazed by tiredness and changing time zones, Iqbal found everything passing by him in a haze of new faces and voices. Everyone wanted to shake his hand and tell him how much they admired him. They all wanted him to eat something or drink something – to such an extent that his bladder, damaged by the abuse it had suffered in the years at the factory, constantly seemed to need emptying. He never minded because every bathroom he visited was a revelation of cleanliness and fragrance compared with the toilets of Muridke and Lahore. It was like living on a different planet rather than a different continent. Sometimes he had to think very hard to remember what life had been like just a week before.

He was taken to visit schools and practised his speech on the children. They stared unashamedly at the small boy who stood before them in his strange national dress, looking so confident and talking in a language they'd never heard before. Their faces were rapt as they listened to Ehsan's translations, unable to believe that anyone so close to their own age could have lived a life so different from theirs.

At Broad Meadows School, Doug Cahn and the Reebok public relations team had organised a campaign to raise awareness of child slavery. The children had written six hundred letters, which they sent off to the Prime Minister of Pakistan, to senior American politicians and to the managers of local carpet stores, urging them not to buy products that had been made by child labourers.

Iqbal wandered around the schools they visited with his mouth hanging open. The children back at Freedom Campus would never believe it when he told them; there were rows of computers for the children to work with, as well as libraries full of books and beautiful sports fields. He wondered how he would ever be able to get an education like these children as long as he had no more than a slate and chalk to work with. There was such a gap between his school experiences and the experiences of the children who were now crowding round him. He couldn't imagine how it could ever be bridged.

At a dinner in an Italian restaurant the night before the award ceremony, around forty people gathered to meet Iqbal and the other recipients and to talk about the awards. A harpist played quietly in the corner of the room and between each tune the enchanted Iqbal would go over to examine the strange instrument close up. The President of Brandeis University was also at the dinner and announced he would be happy to offer Iqbal a scholarship to study at the university once he turned eighteen, if he qualified. When the offer was translated to Iqbal he walked over to the president and hugged him. Maybe this was going to be how he would bridge the gap between where he had come from and where he wanted to get to. Ehsan was always telling him the importance of getting an education; how much finer would it be to get one in America, the most advanced nation in the world?

The award ceremony was being held in the auditorium of Northeastern University and when they arrived at the hall someone introduced Iqbal to a tall, handsome black man called Blair Underwood.

'He's a famous film star,' Ehsan told him after they'd shaken hands.

When the man stood up on stage to make his introduction, Iqbal could tell by the way he spoke and held the audience's attention that he was someone of importance. After a few words about the history of slavery, Blair held out his hand towards the boy on the stage beside him.

'Iqbal Masih,' he boomed, 'leader, inspiration, giant: we honour you with the Reebok Youth in Action Award.'

Iqbal stood up and gave his speech, which was now becoming second nature to him, as he expertly remembered which bits had made the crowd gasp in Sweden, deliberately pausing at the moments of maximum drama. The audience rose to their feet to applaud at the end, just as they had in Stockholm. Iqbal beamed; surely now, he thought, with so many people having been told what was going on, the children would all be freed. He was forgetting how many thousands of miles he'd had to travel in order to deliver the message, and how far they were from the lives of the millions of children who were toiling at exactly the same moment that he was receiving the ovation.

The following day Iqbal was interviewed by ABC News on their 'Person of the Week' segment, and afterwards Ehsan attended a meeting with the officials at Reebok. The deal they agreed on was that $10,000 would go towards Iqbal's education and a further $15,000 would go to the BLLF to help them fund their activities.

'Please keep Iqbal's share here in the US,' Ehsan said. 'Invest it for him and keep it separate from the BLLF funds. That way no one can accuse me of stealing the boy's money.'

'Surely no one would accuse you of that?' The people from Reebok were shocked to think that anyone could accuse a man of Ehsan Khan's reputation of having anything but the best intentions.

'I've made a great many enemies in my country,' Ehsan explained, sadly. 'They would do or say anything to discredit me if they could. They tell me that export orders from Europe and America for carpets made in Pakistan have dropped dramatically since we started our campaign. If it's true, then I'm happy we're having an impact, but it means a lot of people are losing a lot of money. They will eventually get to me and I want Iqbal's money to be safely invested outside the country when that happens.'

'Whatever you want,' they promised.

When the white limousine came to take Ehsan and Iqbal back to the airport, a crowd of people from Reebok and the hotel where he'd been staying came out to wave them off. Not tall enough to see out of the back window, Iqbal knelt up on the soft leather seat to watch the crowd of his new friends waving. The thought that within a few years he might be able to come back as a college student made him want to laugh out loud with joy. He was going to have to work even harder in Mrs Malik's classes if he was going to pass the entry examination, but he was sure he could do it, and Ehsan could help him with his English.

Throughout the drive to the airport, and the wait for the plane, he hardly spoke a word, wanting to soak up every last sight and sound, to commit it all to memory so he would be able to describe America to Fatima. He wanted to be able to tell her about the mountains of food on every restaurant plate, and about how tall the cartons of Coca-Cola were. He wanted to explain about the television screens that flickered everywhere and the music that seemed to play wherever you went, even in lifts. Although he felt sad about leaving America, he couldn't wait to get home to watch Fatima's mouth fall open when he told her that America was even better than on television. He wanted to tell anyone else who would listen, about his great international adventure.

Chapter Fourteen

Home for Easter

Back at the Freedom Campus, Iqbal shared out the many gifts he'd been given with his classmates, whose eyes grew wider and wider with amazement at the sight of so many books and shiny gadgets, and at the splendour of his new Reebok trainers. He told them about the other world he'd visited with its cleanliness, its riches and the kindness of its people. He wanted to tell them about how they should all work to abolish child slavery once and for all, so that Pakistan could become a clean, honest society like the ones he'd glimpsed on his travels. He could tell from their faces they couldn't really picture what he was describing – just as he'd not been able to imagine it when Ehsan had first told him about the trip and pointed America out on his worn old map.

'Now that I've seen how big the world is,' Iqbal told Fatima one evening as they sat, resting with their badminton racquets, 'I can see how small the carpet master was. He used to frighten me so much, but now I've nothing but contempt for him. He lacked all humanity and kindness. He was nothing. I saw that when Ehsan faced up to him.

He was like a mouse in front of a lion. But I've still been afraid that if they got me on my own, which they still do in my dreams, that I would not be strong enough to stand up to them. Now I realise it isn't about how strong my arms might be, or how big their sticks are.'

'What is it about then?' Fatima asked.

'Well, Ehsan says it's about knowing you aren't a slave. If you know that, then they can't make you one. He told me that on my first night in Lahore, but I didn't really understand until I went abroad. In American and Europe no children have to work, not unless they want to.'

Not only was he no longer afraid of his former owner, he now felt even more fearless about going into other factories with Ehsan to free more children, feeling as if he had a huge crowd of people behind him, all clapping and cheering him on. In the first few weeks after his return from America the BLLF closed down a dozen factories, leading the children out to freedom and to their first taste of education.

Iqbal was beginning to believe that the BLLF might be invincible. It seemed that there was hope for the future after all; that it wasn't as black and hopeless as he had once imagined. The more they achieved, the harder he and Ehsan worked, spreading the message around the world and reaching out to as many children as possible. It was no good waiting for world opinion to change and for politicians to suddenly see the light; too many children would grow old and die in slavery before that happened. They had to achieve something concrete every day.

One day Ehsan came across Iqbal walking alone. He had strayed from his normal route on his way home from tea with Fatima in order to wander through a market.

'You must be a little more careful in the streets,' Ehsan warned him, partly pleased to see that Iqbal seemed now to be completely fearless, but alarmed at the same time. 'There are a lot of people who are very angry with us.'

'I'm not afraid of them,' Iqbal assured him, puffing out his chest. 'They keep writing their letters but they don't do anything else. They just want to frighten me into stopping freeing the children, but all they can do is daub slogans on a wall with the blood of some helpless dog.'

'That's true,' Ehsan said, realising Iqbal was quoting back his own sentiments to him. 'But life is cheap in Lahore and if they think they can get to you easily they just might try it. Don't always walk on the same routes around the city and don't draw attention to yourself when you're on your own.'

'I wouldn't do that anyway,' Iqbal protested, affronted that Ehsan might believe he was a show-off.

'I know,' Ehsan smiled at the boy's indignation. 'Just be careful. You're important to the future of this organisation and to the future of Pakistan. You need to look after yourself.'

Iqbal said no more, but inside he was glowing with pride that Ehsan would say such things to him. He'd been telling the truth when he said he wasn't frightened by the threats that had been arriving at the office almost every day – how could they do anything worse to him than the carpet master had done? As Ehsan had said when the first letter had frightened him so much – it was just words.

But Ehsan knew that the people sending the threats and shouting abuse at them at meetings were not their only enemies. He'd been told about a speech made by the president of the Islamabad Carpet Exporters' Association, in which he'd claimed the industry was being victimised by enemy agents who were spreading lies about bonded labour and damaging their business internationally. He knew that the man was talking about the BLLF and that many other people would be listening to such a speech, people with a lot of vested interests in the industry. It would be so easy for people in authority, or with a little money, to remove someone like Iqbal from the street and leave no sign. It cost almost nothing to hire a kidnapper or an assassin. It was a fear he had grown used to living with for himself, but having responsibility for Iqbal reminded him how great the risks were. He didn't know how he would live with himself if anything happened to the boy because he had taught him to hold his head up high and fear no one.

The police would never be interested in hearing about the disappearance of one small boy, especially if that boy had a reputation as a troublemaker. It might even be a policeman who would take on the task of removing him. They wouldn't be intimidated by the fact that the boy had been cheered by thousands of people in Europe and America, that he had appeared on television and in the newspapers. Such people would have no conception of anything outside their own little worlds, where a few extra dollars could make a big difference.

All this worried Ehsan, but he knew Iqbal well enough to realise nothing would stop him from continuing to speak out and free as many children as possible. Having lived with the same fears himself, he knew how they'd always made him more determined and defiant.

He was proud of the boy for that and knew he just had to live with his own fears. Nothing would ever be achieved without taking a few risks. He could hardly insist on curbing Iqbal's new-found freedoms; parents have to let their children go eventually.

Iqbal returned to his studies with a renewed vigour now that he had the chance of going to college in America. If he had asked a lot of questions before, the power of his curiosity was now multiplied a hundred times. Everything he had seen and heard in his travels made him want to learn and understand more. Every adult he came into contact with was left drained and eventually exasperated by his determination to understand the world around him, often painfully reminded of their own lack of answers.

As Easter approached Fatima made her mother invite Iqbal to spend the Sunday with them. She knew Ehsan was going to be out of town, at a conference somewhere on the other side of Pakistan, so she guessed Iqbal would be at a loose end. The request wasn't totally unselfish, however. Fatima loved her mother dearly, but it was nice to have someone her own age around on the days when there wasn't any school to go to. It meant she had someone to do her chores with, and Iqbal always managed to make her laugh so much with his earnest expressions and intense curiosity about everything.

'I would like to very much,' Iqbal replied politely to Mrs Malik's invitation, 'but I haven't seen my family for such a long time and Easter is very important in our village. I'll just go for the day and be back by nightfall, so that I don't miss any school. I don't want to let you or Ehsan down.'

'You worry too much about everyone else,' Mrs Malik told him. 'You don't owe your family anything and I've never had a pupil who's worked as hard in school as you do. Only go to visit your family if you want to, not because you feel you should. Promise me that?'

Iqbal thought for a few moments. 'I want to see my brothers and sister,' he said finally. 'They've probably changed a lot since I was last home.'

'I doubt very much if they'll have changed as much as you have in that time,' Mrs Malik laughed. 'Come by here on your way to the bus and I'll have made you up some food for the journey.'

Iqbal had finally made the decision to make the trip on his own, so that he could spend longer with his family, without them feeling inhibited by Ehsan's presence. He now felt certain that even if the carpet master did try to force him back to work, he would be able to stand up to him. He had overcome so many fears and achieved so much, he could no longer allow the shadows of his childhood to intimidate him. He'd been hit and kicked and shot at by a variety of slave masters while trying to free their workers, and still he survived. What could a man as weak as the carpet master do to him?

Now that the date had been set he was actually looking forward to the trip. Although he had many unhappy memories from his childhood, he had some happy ones too from the time before he was enslaved. He looked forward to spending time with all the friends he and Patras used to swim in the canal with when he was tiny, and to seeing how beautiful his sister had grown since his last visit. Most of all he was looking forward to seeing his mother. He wanted to reassure her that everything had turned out well for him and that she didn't need to worry any more. He didn't think he would be able to explain to her half the things that he'd learned and seen since leaving Muridke, but he felt sure that just seeing him healthy and happy would bring her joy.

Word had been sent to the village, to make sure his family knew he was coming, and he could imagine how all his relatives would arrive, wanting to see what had happened to him and to hear tales of the city. They would all be less inhibited if it was just him there and they would be able to exchange news without having to worry about being polite to an important visitor like Ehsan.

The bus ride out of Lahore was a jolly affair. Many of the passengers were in a holiday mood, some of them carrying baskets of gifts for relatives. He wished he could have afforded to return home with presents for everyone, but he knew they would understand. No one in his family ever expected much.

When the bus deposited him at the end of the road he started the long walk down to the village. As he went he collected a crowd of people who recognised him as Inayat's long-lost son. They were soon followed by others he didn't know who were simply attracted to a crowd. One or two of the older men called out, saying they'd been shown his photograph in the newspapers. He felt so proud of himself. Word had spread that someone interesting was returning to Muridke; boys too young to even remember Iqbal joined the party as it moved on down the road. His cousin, Liaqat, pushed his way to the front and threw his arm round Iqbal's shoulders. Iqbal laughed to see his childhood playmate.

'My father has been asking after you,' Liaqat told him, 'he's heard you're visiting and he wants to see you before you go back to Lahore.'

'I don't know,' Iqbal said, doubtfully, 'there are so many people to see.'

'He's always loved you,' Liaqat insisted. 'Do you remember Faryad?'

He pulled forward an old friend, who put his hand out for Iqbal to shake as they all kept walking. Iqbal wasn't sure if he did remember the other boy. He wasn't even sure he could remember what his Uncle Amanat looked like, but it was nice to think that a senior relative was interested in seeing him.

'My mother will make us some food,' Liaqat went on. 'You have to come.'

'Okay,' Iqbal laughed.

It felt good to be part of a big, loving family. Initially he was pleased to see some familiar faces and to discover they hadn't forgotten him. Then he started to feel embarrassed as the crowd swelled and filled the whole road. After a while, however, he realised it was good, because any lingering fears that the carpet master might make a scene were growing dimmer with every new recruit to the throng.

By the time they were crossing the canal to the village the crowd was far too big to fit into the narrow alleyway that led to the house. Iqbal walked ahead, with a few of his closer relations, while the others fell back, waiting under the trees, talking and passing the rest of the afternoon peacefully now the excitement had moved on. Liaqat and Faryad were pushed to the back by the grown-ups.

As Iqbal arrived at the gate to the courtyard of the house his mother appeared with her arms outstretched and tears flowing down her cheeks.

'My son has returned,' she wailed dramatically and the male relatives fell back respectfully to allow her to throw her arms around her long-lost son, clutching him to her. Iqbal allowed her to hold him for as long as she wanted, drinking in the familiar smell of her body, which he'd missed for so long, but never forgotten.

When she finally released him he shook hands very formally with Patras who had grown into a young man with a responsible job on a food stall, while Sobya hung back and watched. Both of them looked dazed by the size of the crowd and seemed unsure what to say. Aslam, his half-brother, came forward and shook his hand as if they were the closest of friends. Iqbal responded in the same vein. He bore his half-brother no grudges, he had just done what he thought was right.

As the crowd filtered down still further to get across the courtyard and in through the doors, there was a great deal of jostling for position. In the end Inayat had to lay down the law as to who was allowed inside to sit on the beds and who must wait outside. If someone had to leave the room, someone else would be allowed to take their place. The heat from the crush of bodies rose as the afternoon progressed and more and more people sidled up to tell Iqbal their news and to ask if there was anything he could do to help with their various problems.

It didn't seem strange to him at all that family members were suddenly treating him as if he were an elder, rather than a small boy, as if he had come back ordained into the church. He did feel that he was older and wiser than all of them now. He felt like he'd been to places and seen things that had opened his eyes. No one in the village seemed to have changed since the day he left; it was suddenly clear to him how badly they needed the help of teachers and doctors and other educated people like Ehsan and Mrs Malik. He tried to answer their questions as best he could, but all the time he was telling himself that one day he would come back with a proper education and he would really have something to offer them.

Eventually it was time for him to start his journey home, stopping off on the way to visit his Uncle Amanat, and pay his respects.

So that was how Iqbal came to be on the way back to Lahore from Muridke on the fateful day when the man with the gun stepped out from behind the tree, took aim at the three small boys on the bike and fired.

CHAPTER FIFTEEN

THE ASSASSINATION OF A CHILD

Even before the last echoes of the explosions had died away, the man with the gun was already running from the scene. The squawking of the disturbed birds circling in the sky above was replaced by the wails of the two frightened friends as they picked themselves up from the dust and tried to work out what had happened and where they were damaged. There was a lot of blood on Faryad's arm where some of the shots had pierced the flesh, making it hard to see how many pellets had hit him. Liaqat was also splattered with blood but as he checked the various parts of his body he realised none of it was his.

His father's curry and rice was spread all over the ground where it had fallen from Iqbal's fingers and Liaqat's first thoughts were of how angry his mother would be to hear that all her efforts at cooking had been wasted. It was a few seconds before either of the boys realised Iqbal had not stood up with them. He was lying still and silent, his body twisted awkwardly round the fallen bicycle. His white shirt had turned crimson and the stain was spreading.

The screams of the boys travelled for miles across the previously deserted landscape, bringing people running from every horizon. Amanat was the first to reach them, gasping for breath after such sudden exertions in the air-less warmth of the evening, his eyes wide with fear at what he was going to find. His initial relief at finding his own son alive and unhurt was quickly replaced with distress for the fallen Iqbal.

Everyone in the area had heard of the work the boy had been doing in freeing the children from the factories and brick kilns; it didn't surprise Amanat that someone would want him dead. He knelt beside the bike and turned Iqbal's face towards him. The eyes were as wide open as they had been when they had first seen the gun barrel pointing at them. They didn't blink.

When Amanat lifted the light little body it was as limp as a pile of rags. Others joined them, as if from nowhere, abandoning their flocks of animals as they made their way slowly back to Amanat's house. By the time they got there someone had found a friend who had a rusty farm truck, which could be used to carry the body to the police station. The women bound up Faryad's arm to stop the bleeding. He looked pale but seemed not to be in any danger. The boys were silent with shock as everyone babbled around them.

All the men and boys at the house climbed into the van for the trip. Everyone was still talking at once, making different suggestions about what they should do, giving different theories about who might be responsible. Not very much ever happened in those quiet fields and no one wanted to miss out on being part of such a drama. The women in the house clucked and tutted at the foolishness of men and the unkindness of the fates as they watched the van bumping away towards the road, its dim headlights cutting only a small swathe in the darkness that had now fallen.

The guard who opened the gate at the police station kept his gun at the ready. He was uneasy about letting so many people into the compound at once in the dark. Other policemen were coming out of the office area to see what all the shouting was about. Any distraction that broke the tedium of the night shift was welcome. Even the commander came strutting across towards the van as it pulled up on the far side, straightening his cap and puffing out his chest as he went. It was the same man who had once taken Iqbal back to the carpet master, although he had quite forgotten the incident; there had been so many more since. The prisoners in the cell came to the bars to watch, pleased to have the police momentarily distracted from shouting abuse at them.

'What's going on?' the commander demanded.

'A body from a shooting,' the guard from the gate informed him.

'All right, get back to your post,' the commander instructed, giving the open gates a nervous look. He always felt better when he was behind locked gates at night, or in a locked car.

The small crowd, which had been standing round the back of the van, peering in, parted as he cut a path through with his swagger stick.

'Oh,' he said, unable to hide the disappointment in his voice. 'It's a kid. Where did it happen?'

'Out in the fields,' one of the men who'd travelled with the body answered.

'Any witnesses?' He stared at Iqbal's face but didn't recognise him, seeing just another dead street urchin.

'Just two other kids and the boy's uncle, but he was a long way off.'

'Bring them to my office,' he instructed his men, 'and put the body in the corner.'

The officers lifted the stiffening body out and laid it on the ground where the commander had indicated, while the men who'd accompanied it escorted the boys to the office. Once inside, the commander took his time removing his cap, arranging his papers, making phone calls and drinking a cup of tea, enjoying the moment of drama before turning to them. They all waited respectfully.

Once he was ready, he asked them what had happened and listened, his eyes closed and his fingers steepled thoughtfully in front of his pursed lips. He took no notes.

An hour or two later the gates of the police station opened again to allow the van to drive out with all the men and boys from the fields on board. As soon as the gates were closed once more the police station went back to its sleepy night-time routines, with Iqbal's body resting, temporarily forgotten, in the corner. Someone on the next shift could decide what to do with that.

Although the news took a while to spread from the fields, once it had reached Lahore it picked up speed. By late morning Ehsan had received a call in the hotel where he was staying for the conference in Islamabad. He was in his room with a lawyer at the time, distracted by their discussion and only half concentrating on the words he was hearing from the phone, staring out the window at the mountains. The man on the other end of the line had to repeat what he was saying several times before Ehsan was able to take it in, and it still seemed unbelievable.

'They wanted to say you'd killed him for publicity,' his informant told him. 'Just to get you in trouble. They didn't realise you were at the other end of the country. Now they're trying to make up new stories.'

'Where is he now?' Ehsan wanted to know.

'They left him in the police station.'

'He's on his own?'

'I think so.'

'They'll just put him out with the rubbish. I'll get back as soon as I can.'

Ehsan didn't have a car with him; he'd come up on the bus. There was no other way back. It was going to be hours before he could get there, hours that would be an agony as he thought back over the many ways he could have made things happen differently. He could have taken Iqbal with him to Islamabad, or stayed in Lahore himself and gone out to Muridke with him. Or he could have insisted a couple of men took Iqbal there and back in a car. There were so many things he could have done. He had known a lot of people who had been killed, but he had never felt like this before. He wondered if this unbearable sadness would ever fade.

As dawn broke the police commander still had no idea the body in his compound was anything more than another dhalit nobody. He'd gone home and was just settling down for a sleep when his phone rang and he was informed of who the small boy riddled with bullets was.

'This is going to cause trouble,' he was told. 'They will use him as an excuse to discredit everyone they can.'

Realising immediately that the people who were calling him were serious, he was back in his uniform and in his office within half an hour, having sent a patrol car out to fetch Liaqat and Faryad back in.

Deprived of sleep and seeing more trouble coming, the commander was not in a good mood by the time they arrived. The boys were soon made aware that if they weren't careful they would be in the cell next door and charged with the murder of their cousin and friend.

Neither of them had slept well and they were still in

shock from the events of the night before. The questions the commander kept firing at them confused them further and his anger made them think that if they didn't find the right answers they were going to be beaten.

Then he offered to make their lives easier by telling them what their new testimony should be. At first they didn't understand what was being asked of them, but spending a few hours in the cell next door gave them time to think.

'You're right,' they told the commander when they were brought back into his office. 'It was Ashraf.'

'Excellent,' the commander smiled, genuinely pleased he'd managed to find a solution to the mystery. 'So let's take your statement in front of witnesses.'

There were plenty of people in the station that day who were happy to crowd into the commander's office to witness the telling of the new story. They heard how the three boys were cycling out to take Amanat his supper when they came upon a local farm worker, Ashraf, pleasuring himself with a donkey in the field. Iqbal, the other two boys confirmed, had made fun of the man, not realising he had a gun. Angry at being interrupted and mocked, Ashraf had let loose a volley of shots that had killed Iqbal and wounded his friend.

The boys knew Ashraf; everyone in the area did. He was easily confused and would have trouble remembering whether it had happened or not. They were grateful to the commander for giving them a way to please him and to ensure he didn't need to put them back in the cell as the heat of the day built up. They felt bad about involving poor, simple Ashraf, but they would have said anything to escape from police custody. And, after all, Ashraf wouldn't really understand what was going on.

Another patrol car was sent out into the fields to arrest Ashraf and bring him to the station.

When Ehsan finally arrived at the police station he was afraid he would be too late, that they would have disposed of the evidence before he got there. He needn't have worried; the body was still lying where they'd first dumped it, waiting for someone to decide what should be done next. Ehsan walked briskly across the compound, ignored the gaggle of policemen congregating behind him as he knelt down beside the body of his little friend and bent forward to kiss his forehead, causing a cloud of flies to rise angrily into the air.

The heat of the sun meant Iqbal was as warm as if his heart had still been pumping blood through his veins. It was as if he was just sleeping, except no one had taken the trouble to close his eyes. Ehsan gently lowered the lids with the tips of his fingers and knelt for a while, lost in sad thoughts. He had to fly to Europe the next day for another conference and it felt like he was deserting Iqbal when he needed him. The boy looked so alone and abandoned on the ground. But there was nothing else he could do for him now and the conference was important, a way of spreading the message to many hundreds more people. He felt as if his heart was being torn from his chest as he stood up and walked away, and the flies settled back down onto Iqbal.

'He should be taken to his family in Muridke,' Ehsan told the commander, 'so they can bury him decently before he cooks in the sun.'

'We need an autopsy first,' the commander said. 'We must establish the truth of what has happened here.'

'Will an autopsy help do that?' Ehsan asked, his eyebrows arched. 'No one is going to be worried about the truth here.'

'The family can bury him as soon as the doctors and scientists have finished their work,' the commander went on, as if he hadn't heard Ehsan's comment. He could see the advantage of getting the evidence underground before anyone else came snooping around, asking more awkward questions, but he couldn't afford to have anyone say he hadn't done everything by the book. This was the sort of case that was likely to have ramifications. He'd met troublemakers like Ehsan Khan before; they never stopped with their questions and accusations; they could cause a great deal of damage to a man's career if they weren't handled right. The commander wanted to make sure there were other people to give the answers than him when the time came.

Ashraf was slumped in the cell with the other prisoners as Ehsan walked past. He had no idea what was happening outside and didn't understand what he was being accused of.

The story of the donkey was spreading and mutating as it went. In the weeks to come anyone who wanted to discredit any suggestion that the murder might have been instigated by the carpet manufacturers was able to quote the story with a knowing smirk and everyone understood that things might not be as they seemed.

News of Iqbal's death reached America and the children who had met him in their schools, and who had written letters lobbying for an end to child labour, were struck by the reality of a world they could barely imagine; a world where a child who had seemed like one of them could be assassinated and no one would instigate an enquiry. Iqbal, who had seemed so full of life and energy, was dead, and life just kept on as normal.

In Boston the children he had met held a candlelit vigil in his memory and wept, shocked by the brutality of a world beyond their own experience. The myth of Iqbal, the freer of slaves, had spread far outside his native country and would continue to grow whatever his enemies might do to try to discredit him at home.

The autopsy left Iqbal's body cut to pieces, nothing of use having been discovered, no mysteries solved, no conclusions reached, and that was how he was returned to his family. They welcomed him with loud wailing and a rending of garments. To have their own martyred saint in the family made every member feel proud and they wanted to howl their grief to the world, to let everyone know just how great their little relative had been. Patras, Sobya and Liaqat were all strangely silent. They were overwhelmed by the enormity of what had happened to their brother and cousin, lost in their own thoughts and unable to join in the loud exhibition of grief.

Inayat seemed inconsolable, barely able to stand without the support of her older son and stepson. As she sobbed, the other women of the village crowded round to wail with her in support. Iqbal's body, covered in a sheet so that only his face was visible, was put on display and the whole village filed past to look at the boy who'd made Muridke famous. The funeral procession the next day collected a mighty crowd by the time it reached the Christian grave-yard at the back of the village. They had their very own hero to celebrate and mourn; how many villages could claim such an honour?

Children who'd once worked in the brick kilns but had been led to freedom by Iqbal, came with bricks they'd made specially and imprinted with their hands, laying them on the grave in a makeshift monument. Within days they'd all been stolen by people who wanted to build walls on top of their houses.

★

The death of a small dhalit boy in the middle of a field in Pakistan would normally have meant nothing. The family would have mourned for a few days and then moved on, but this was a small boy who had become a symbol for millions of others. His murder caused reverberations in embassies and government buildings all over the world, making people think and talk about a system that could allow such a thing to happen. It was the last thing that anyone who worked within the system wanted.

By the time the tale had reached the very highest political echelons in Pakistan the story invented within the police compound had been given one more twist. The prime minister, when questioned about the murder on television, suggested that Iqbal had been shot by an irate farmer when he, Iqbal, was caught copulating with the farmer's donkey. The image fitted with another myth that was being circulated that Iqbal had not been a boy at all but a midget, who Ehsan had been passing off as a child for publicity purposes. The prime minister only knew what she had been told and it was impossible to know at which stage of its journey the story took this final grotesque turn.

On hearing the rumour that Iqbal was actually a mature nineteen-year-old, Ehsan's colleagues in Sweden went back to the doctor who had ordered all the X-rays of Iqbal when he was visiting, and the doctor was happy to vouch for the fact that he was still only a young boy, certainly no more than thirteen at the time of his death. But it was too late to stop the story from circulating anyway; it had been fostered and spread by people who didn't want to have created a child martyr.

But ultimately it didn't matter what lies the political and business grapevines propagated, the story of the courageous small boy had already taken too firm a grip in too many minds to ever let go. Tales of the thousands of children he'd led to safety grew more prolifically than slurs of how Ehsan had exploited him and cheated his family of their rightful money. Slowly but surely, the positive stories began to outweigh the negative.

There was little Ehsan could do about the national press, but whenever stories accusing him of treating Iqbal dishonourably appeared in the international press, he would sue the papers and they would be forced to retract their stories and pay damages to the BLLF.

The political and business elite in Pakistan had no credibility left in the matter; no one believed the tales they told any more but everyone wanted to believe that one small boy would have the courage to face his persecutors and to then go to the rescue of thousands of fellow sufferers.

Ehsan didn't change his plans to travel to Europe for the conference after Iqbal's death. There was nothing else he could do for the boy now. He didn't want to be part of the mourning process. He wanted to remember his friend without the crowds and the histrionics. Iqbal would have understood; the most important thing was to keep working, to keep spreading the word, to keep moving towards a day when it would be unthinkable that any child should be forced to live and die as Iqbal had.

Ehsan was in his hotel in Stockholm when he received a call from a colleague in Lahore.

'You mustn't come back,' the man told him.

'What do you mean?' Ehsan asked.

'They've said that if you ever return to Pakistan you'll be arrested at the airport for treason.'

'Treason?'

'If you come back you'll be hanged within days,' the friend informed him. 'This time they mean it.'

For a moment Ehsan felt a rush of fury. How dare anyone force him to stay away from his home country? How could they accuse him of treason when all he wanted to do was to make Pakistan a better place for all its citizens, not just the rich and powerful? He reminded himself that he had been threatened many times before and the threats had vanished into thin air when he had faced up to them. It was only after several days of phone calls to other friends and contacts that he realised this time it was true. If he tried to set foot in the country they would arrest him immediately and once he was out of sight there would be nothing to stop them killing him, either with or without a fair trial.

He felt a terrible sadness overcome him. He loved his country and never felt comfortable anywhere else in the world. Was he really doomed now to wander the world outside his own homeland? His friends warned him to stay out of sight. Wherever he went, they told him, his enemies would be looking for him.

His enemies had finally lost patience and decided they couldn't allow him to do any more damage to them or their friends in the business community. They believed that if they could silence him, as they had silenced Iqbal, there would be no one else in Lahore who would speak up and be listened to by the outside world. If they could just have a little time to let things calm down they would be able to get business back to usual, winning back customers who had been frightened off with words like 'child labour' and 'slavery'. It was all a matter of rebuilding confidence in the market. Ehsan swore to himself that just because he was being forced to go into hiding, didn't mean he wasn't going to continue to work for the cause in any way he could. Iqbal Masih's name would never be forgotten.

Afterword

I was introduced to Ehsan in London by a Pakistani film-maker who was interested in making a movie of Iqbal's short life. The filmmaker and I waited for him in the incongruous surroundings of Belgravia and Ehsan appeared out of the smart Sloane Street crowds as if from nowhere, with his trademark flowing white shirt and moustache, a strange hybrid of flamboyance and anonymity.

All through lunch he paid virtually no attention to his food or the elegant restaurant, wanting only to talk about Iqbal and about the cause that has taken up virtually every waking moment of his life for years. He never smiled or laughed. The stories he told of how life is for the hundreds of thousands of people who spend their childhoods in servitude shocked me, and I was moved by the way he had dedicated his own life so completely to spreading the message and saving as many children as he could.

Still forced to live in hiding in Europe, he couldn't come back to Pakistan with us, but he promised to help us to meet the right people and see the places where

Iqbal lived his short life while we were there. After lunch he vanished into the crowds, just as quickly as he had appeared, taking calls as he went.

By the time we arrived in Lahore many of the BLLF supporters had been rounded up and sent to jail where they were beyond our prying questions, but still we were able to find people wanting to talk and show us what had happened. Each day rumours filtered out to us of how the prisoners were being beaten, but no one could find a way to reach them.

We visited the homes, offices and schools where many who knew and loved Iqbal still live and work. We visited carpet factories where children continue to labour and we ate in the restaurant where Iqbal and Ehsan had eaten. We saw all the places where he had lived and slept and died. Everyone had favourite stories they wanted to tell about the boy and some of them have become so embroidered through the years it was hard to tell what was fact and what was myth.

Films can take decades to get off the ground and it seemed important to me that Iqbal's story should be told as often and as widely as possible, so I decided to write his story. Hopefully the film will soon be made and will carry his message still further. I have tried to imagine what really happened, using all the fragments of his life that I was able to glean, but in a way it is the myth that is the true story.

About the Author

Andrew Crofts is one of the UK's leading ghostwriters. His books include a string of number one bestsellers, including *Sold*, *The Little Prisoner*, *The Kid*, and *Just a Boy*, and most recently *For a House Made of Stone* (Vision).